Dick Sutphen's
Lighting
The Light Within

Valley of the Sun Publishing, Box 38, Malibu, CA 90265

Books by Dick Sutphen:

Simon & Schuster Pocket Books:
You Were Born Again To Be Together
Past Lives, Future Loves
Unseen Influences
Predestined Love (1988)

Valley of the Sun Publishing:
Past-Life Therapy In Action (co-written with
        Lauren Leigh Taylor)
Master of Life Manual
Enlightenment Transcripts
A.T. & How To Instantly Read People
Sedona: Psychic Energy Vortexes
Poet: 1970–1985
Rattlesnake Karma

For information, write:
Valley of the Sun Publishing
Box 38
Malibu, CA 90265

Front cover photo of sunset: Richard Ruehs, Tempe, Arizona. Photo of Dick Sutphen: Agoura Artists, Agoura Hills, California. Back cover photo collage: "Endless Journey" ©1986 by Ruth Terrill, 9700 Alpine Road, Box 120, Star Route 2, La Honda, California 94020.

First Printing: August 1987
Additional copies of **Lighting The Light Within** are available by mail for $3.95 each. Send check or money order plus $1.50 per order for postage and handling to: Valley of the Sun Publishing, Box 38, Malibu, California 90265. A catalog of over 350 tapes and books is also available.

ISBN: 0-87554-154-2
Library of Congress Catalog Card Number: 87-50555

For Hunter Shane Sutphen

Contents

This book is an introduction to the **Master of Life** teachings of **Dick Sutphen.** The chapters are excerpts from his many books, tapes, seminar workshops, appearance talks, and magazine articles. Dick has nothing to join and no ongoing program to promote. He publishes *Master of Life*, a full-color quarterly magazine; each issue is read by over half a million people, making it the largest circulation New Age publication in the country. It is sent free to book/tape buyers and those who attend his seminars. (See the back of this book for information.)

1.

Lighting The Light Within

Metaphysical teachers, human-potential trainers, psychologists, and psychiatrists are in agreement on one thing: Your attitudes and problems go back to a **cause.** Somewhere in your past, you had experiences that resulted in your becoming the person you are today. These experiences are the foundation of your current reality.

Problem Examples	Attitude Examples
Weight problems	Rebellious/Conformist
Marital Conflicts	Liberal/Conservative
Lack of a Relationship	Responsible/Irresponsible
Accidents	Assertive/Meek
Loneliness	Shy/Outgoing
Sickness	Brave/Cowardly
Disease	Generous/Selfish
Guilt	Optimistic/Pessimistic
Monetary Hardship	Proud/Humble
Unfulfilled Desires	Honest/Untrustworthy
Low Self-Esteem	Courteous/Uncivil

Psychologists, psychiatrists and most human-potential trainers will assist you to find the cause of your attitudes and problems, if they are the result of experiences from the time of your birth up to the present ... in this life. These mental-health professionals do not normally accept reincarnation and karma as the basis of reality. As a result, they find the cause less than half the time.

The metaphysical teacher accepts reincarnation and karma, and so is usually much more successful in locating the cause, which will be an event or a series of events, often experienced in past lives. By exploring the karmic chain of cause and effect with regression and sophisticated altered-state-of-consciousness technology, it is often possible to quickly attain an awareness of your current **influences, motivations** and **restrictions.**

*The next step
in human
evolution
has to be*

*the mastery of
what
until now
has been*

*the unexplained
potentials
of the mind.*

2.

Love And Joy/Tears And Growth

Three Case History Dialogues from the book
"Enlightenment Transcripts."

There is a Zen koan that asks, "A man hangs on by one hand to a root, suspended over a sheer precipice. Can he open his grip and let go?" What a spiritual-potential seminar like the **Master of Life Training** can do is to hang a man on that precipice; but there is the root that brought him there in the first place, and to that he will cling with desperation. Only he himself can relinquish that grip when he is ready. **Master of Life** awareness gets you ready to let go, but it is you who has to let go.

The following are three of the 36 case history dialogues that make up part of **Enlightenment Transcripts.** The dialogues are taken from training room tape recordings and are primarily in response to an altered-state session, an exercise, or talk. As a result of being hung over the precipice, the seminar participant decides to question his own situation.

Aura

I was talking to the entire group about guilt. "Guilt is

not just something that happened in the past. Everyone in this room is dealing with different kinds of guilt. Guilt is the primary manipulation trap that people use on each other, especially within families and close relationships. There are only two reasons for someone to attempt to make you feel guilty: 1. to control you; 2. to hurt you. Neither is worthy of your consideration. Here are a few of my favorite lines: 'How can you treat me like this?' 'It was your fault that I was upset and didn't get enough sleep!' 'I've been waiting by the phone all week for you to call.' And if you feel guilty, don't blame them. Blame yourself for allowing someone to manipulate you.

"It's easiest to break guilt down into three kinds: **1. current guilt; 2. long-standing guilt; 3. philosophical guilt.** Examples of current guilt might be not spending enough time with the kids or not calling your parents as often as you feel you should. Examples of long-standing guilt would be guilt over leaving your ex-wife, or guilt over refusing to allow your ailing father to move in with you when he asked to. An example of philosophical guilt would be not tithing to the church when you feel it is your responsibility to do so.

"Guilt is an attempt to make right in the present something you did or think you are doing wrong. Guilt always inhibits you and you dwell upon the guilt, generating more and more negative programming to your subconscious mind each time you think about it.

"But let's deal with the guilts one at a time. Since no one can change the past, long-standing guilt is always inappropriate. You can't undo what is done, and to dwell upon it destroys the present and future. But current guilt and philosophical guilt you can do something about if you choose to. You can choose to support a viewpoint of being bad. You want to gain self-acceptance and you can't do this when you feel you are bad, unless you make yourself feel

10

guilty. Guilt is an internal debit and credit system. Once you've felt guilty long enough, it balances or justifies your actions. You can feel okay with yourself. The problem is that you usually just do the same thing all over again. Guilt is often a never-ending spiral unless you decide to end it. From a karmic perspective, guilt is one of the most destructive of all emotions."

Aura was a very pretty woman in her late thirties, dressed in a long cotton dress in a style that had been popular with the hippies in the sixties and early seventies. She wore several kinds of metaphysical necklaces around her neck and silver and turquoise bracelets on both arms. "I'd like nothing more than to let go of the guilt that haunts me, but how do you do it?" she asked.

"It has to start with an awareness of guilt and how it works," I said. "Then, if it's a current or philosophical guilt, you're going to have to explore the clarity of your intent. In other words, decide what is important and then act. If your guilt is long-standing and you cannot do anything to remedy the situation, label it 'experience,' file it away, and go back to it only as a point of reference."

"But I can't let go of it. My guilt is long-standing and haunts me night and day. When I was younger, I took a lot of drugs. Four years ago, my daughter was born mentally retarded. Every day, she is a living reminder of my guilt. I love her more than anything in the world, and I've rearranged my whole life to take care of her. But when I think about how I robbed her of the life she could have had, it just kills me." Tears were rolling down Aura's cheeks and she couldn't hide her trembling.

"Aura, did you know when you took the drugs that they would someday affect a child you might have?" I asked.

"No, I didn't. I really didn't," she responded. "But I certainly should have considered the possibility."

"Aura, you have an understanding of karma. It is never

11

one-sided. The soul that entered your daughter's body deliberately chose the circumstances as a way to resolve her own karma, and to offer you the opportunity to resolve yours."

"If only I could believe that," she said.

"Do you accept karma as what is?" I asked. She nodded. I continued, "Then you have to accept that there is no halfway karma. **All** is karma or this is a random universe and there is no meaning to life other than what you see. Would you like to explore your relationship in regression?"

"Oh, yes, please," she said.

After inducing an altered state of consciousness, I told Aura, "Somewhere in the memory banks of your subconscious mind are memories that relate to your current situation with your daughter. And I want you to let go of the physical and flow back into your mental memories of previous incarnations to observe firsthand how the past relates to the present. It is time to attain an awareness of the karmic relationship, and to better understand that which influences, restricts and motivates you now."

I gave Aura the regression instructions, then said, "The impressions are beginning to form. When you can, I want you to speak up and tell me what you perceive."

"Riding on horseback . . . going very fast. There's a man in a uniform of some kind and . . . oh, no! Somebody shot him. He's fallen off the horse and is just lying there, not moving. Other riders are coming; they are dressed in different uniforms. They look at him and laugh, and just ride away."

"Are you the man who has been shot?" I asked.

"I think so."

"Let's move forward in time until something else happens, if it does. On the count of three, you'll be there. One, two, three. What's happening now?"

12

"Someone else, another man in the same kind of uniform as mine. He's helping me. The bullet wound is to the left side of my stomach and he is attempting to stop the bleeding. He seems to be wounded, too, but he is putting me on the horse now, taking me somewhere."

"All right, let's move forward in time until we can find out how this comes out. Move to an important situation in the future. One, two, three."

"I'm in a bed in the ward of an old-fashioned hospital. A nurse is telling me I won't ever be able to walk again. The bullet hit my spine and my legs are paralyzed. My friend—the one who saved me—is there too. Oh, God, I'm just going crazy. I'm screaming at them to shoot me right now and put me out of my misery. The nurse doesn't care. She's just watching and then she just walks away." Aura breaks off for a moment, tears slipping down her cheeks. Sobbing, she continues, "My friend says he'll help me. His parents have a farm and we'll go there."

"All right, I want you to let go of this. Now, on the count of three and not before the count of three, without pain and without emotion, I want you to move forward to a time a few weeks before you died in this past life we are now examining. You have not yet crossed over into spirit. It will be a few weeks prior to your death. And I want you to attain an overview of all that happened of importance up to this time. One, two, three."

Aura was silent for a moment or two, her eyes moving rapidly under her closed lids, an indication that dream-like impressions were taking place. "I'm much older now and in a wheelchair in a studio-like room. Clay is everywhere—clay molds, dishes, cups, figures. Why, yes, I've learned pottery. I'm a potter, that's what I do. Funny, my hair is white at the temples and I'm probably about 50 years old. I seem to cough a lot."

"What happened to your friend, the one who saved

you?" I asked.

"Hollis is here. Probably in the next room or outside," she replied.

"Then he stayed with you and helped you all these years?"

"Oh, yes, we're still on the farm. His parents died and now he runs it with his own children. But he has always helped me. I learned to be a potter and my work sells well. I help out in that way." She was silent for a while.

After awakening Aura, I said, "Can you understand now, Aura? Your daughter took care of you in a previous life, and in this life, you have been given the opportunity to repay an old debt."

"Yes, I see that," she responded. "But she didn't shoot me in the past life. In our present situation, I took the drugs and she is suffering."

"Aura, from a karmic perspective, if there is karma resulting from the drug taking, you are certainly paying it off every day of your life, considering your situation with your daughter. But it was also the drug taking that set up the circumstances for mental retardation. This may be why your daughter chose to come through you. Her need to experience this tragic circumstance is due to her desire for spiritual growth, which will result from this form of balance."

"Like what? How can you possibly justify such an idea?" she asked.

"Karma is never one-sided, Aura. But there is no way for us to know the karmic implications."

"Well, can you just make something up that could help me understand?" she almost begged.

"All right. Let's say that the soul currently inhabiting your daughter's body has become very proud over a series of lifetimes, so proud that it is detrimental to spiritual growth. Maybe the soul has been open to helping others

14

in many lifetimes, such as the one you just explored. But this soul has grown far too proud to personally accept help from others. How does the soul regain balance? Maybe by coming into a life of total dependency. That is one potential.

"Do you see? It could be any of millions of potentials. Maybe in a past life, the soul turned away from someone in a similar position, or maybe the soul was so fearful of mental retardation that the only way to understand and rise above the fear was to experience the affliction."

The tears were now flowing down Aura's face, faster than before. A support team member handed her a tissue. "Thank you," she whispered to me.

(Note: many of the dialogues in **Enlightenment Transcripts** relate to other dialogues. In the following situation, Neal is responding to a regression in which Joan has found the cause of her excessive pride and tendency to blame others.)

Neal

"What do you think about Joan's experience?" I asked the group. Neal put up his hand, and when recognized, asked, "What is the value in her knowing all that?"

"Joan's conscious and subconscious mind have been out of alignment, causing her to be very judgmental. Her past experiences have generated fears that have blocked her from expressing unconditional love. Understanding your fears is one way of rising above them."

Neal seemed to ponder the answer for a while. He was in his early twenties, and dressed in a sweater and jeans. "What are other ways to rise above your fear?" he asked.

"Well, to begin with, you must realize that every problem is rooted in fear. Most of the powerful new therapies do not believe in mental illness, but contend that unhappy and neurotic people are not satisfying their needs and that they have developed negative patterns of thinking and acting. This results in anguish and suffering for them, and usually for those close to them.

"There is no way to heal a mind, so medical therapy does not relate. What is needed is an understanding of the fears behind the negative thoughts and actions, and an understanding of the individual's needs. This is followed by re-education, which is learning the skill of choosing wisely between behavior that will result in **harmony,** opposed to behavior which will result in **disharmony.** Basically, this is the ability to **reason.**

"So, if your life isn't working; if you have symptoms such as depression, anxiety, phobias, and stomach ulcers; if you drink or do drugs to escape; if you're experiencing guilt, repression, jealousy, possessiveness, hatred, anger, tension, greed, inhibition, stress, envy, or paranoia . . . you are experiencing irrational fears and your essential needs are not being fulfilled. The list of symptoms is endless, but whatever they are, you can help yourself to resolve them."

"But what about Joan? Her problem went back to a past life," Neal asked.

"The past life may have been the cause, but the need relates to love," I replied. "All human beings have the same physiological and psychological needs, but we vary in our ability to fulfill them. Psychiatry is concerned with two basic psychological needs: 1. the need to love and be loved, and 2. the need to feel worthwhile to ourselves and to others.

"Regarding the need to love, you must be involved with other people—one person at the very minimum. We all must have one person who loves us and whom we love. If we don't have this critical person in our life, we will not be able to fulfill our basic needs, and mental symptoms will result.

"Regarding the need to feel worthwhile to yourself and to others, you must maintain a satisfactory standard of behavior. This means that you must correct yourself when you are wrong. If your conduct is below your standard, you must correct it or you will suffer, just as if you had no one to love and no one to love you.

"This is why much of this seminar is about exploring your fears and working to remove the blocks to your expression of unconditional love. It is also about exploring your behavior to decide if it is disharmonious and if you need to change it.

"I encourage immediate changes in **behavior** which will quickly lead to a change in **attitude,** which can lead to fulfilling your needs. **You don't have to change how you feel about something to affect it, if you are willing to change what you are doing.** Change begins with action. Karma is action, and wisdom erases karma.

"And remember what I said earlier: Nothing about ourselves can be changed until it is first recognized and accepted. So, to recognize what you really are behind all your masks, you must ask yourself a lot of questions. Answers are never difficult if you stop avoiding the questions you need to ask yourself. So, in regard to any fear, there are four questions:

"1. What is the real fear?

"2. What needs do I have that are not being met?

"3. What am I doing that creates disharmony?

"4. How can I change my behavior to create more harmony?"

"Okay, what about resistance?" Neal asked. "Back when you were talking about resisting what is, I realized that I resist my boss something terrible. I mean, everything he says just grates on me. I dwell on it. I just hate him for some reason and I don't even know why."

"All right, Neal, close your eyes and just trust the first thoughts that come into your mind. What is the real fear behind your resistance to your boss?"

"I don't know," he immediately replied.

17

"Yes, you do, Neal, and you're not playing the game. Just trust the thoughts that come in."

"That he'll win!" Neal blurted out, loudly.

"What does that mean?" I asked.

"Well, he's just so damned smug. He's such a know-it-all, always looking down his nose at me. If I didn't do something, he'd think he is superior and he isn't. He's an idiot."

"So the fear is that you'll lose because you didn't get to be right, and get to be superior over him?" Neal grimaced at the way I viewed his response. "All right, Neal, second question: What needs do you have that are not being met?"

"Ah, I'd like some respect for my abilities. All I ever get from him is disapproval."

"Neal, any time you or anyone else gets upset with anyone about anything, your expectations are in conflict with **what is.** You have expectations of approval or control, and when these expectations aren't fulfilled, you get upset. You want to attain your boss's approval or control his actions. Neither is right. And what is, is that your boss is a superior-acting know-it-all! Okay, third question: What are you doing that creates disharmony?"

"I verbally cut at him whenever I can, in areas that don't contradict his authority. I keep it personal, that way he can't get me fired for my attitude toward my work," he said, with obvious pride.

"Okay, Neal, last question: How can you change your behavior to create more harmony?"

"Well, I guess I could let him be right and just do my job. I could just accept that he is what he is. Based upon what I've heard in here, I'm just making it worse by resisting because I'm programming my subconscious mind with negativity."

"What about that?" I asked.

"Well, I guess it isn't logical to make things worse for yourself. It's kinda dumb, too."

18

Turning to the rest of the participants, I said, "So the idea here is **conscious detachment based upon awareness ... based upon wisdom.** And I contend that once Neal changes his behavior, he will soon change how he feels about his work relationship. He may not ever like his boss, but his boss will cease to be an issue. Remember, a change in behavior will quickly lead to a change in attitude. You don't have to change how you feel about something to affect it if you are willing to change what you are doing."

Sunny

As Sunny spoke, she began rubbing the back of her neck, which is body language indicating anxiety related to her words. She was in her mid-twenties, dressed in jeans and a white cotton beach jacket with the collar turned up.

"I've been forced, through a shifting of assignments in my office, to work with a woman who drives me to distraction. She isn't superior to me nor am I to her, but she acts like she is the boss. She does everything she can to put me down and to discredit me to our boss. She's several years older and I'm afraid she is going to hurt my career in the film business."

"How do you respond to her?" I asked.

"I try to keep it in and remain perfectly nice. Just like the mask you talked about. And I've listened to everything that has been said in this seminar, and I know a lot of it applies to this situation, but I just don't see how the awareness is really going to change anything."

"What is it you see in her that you recognize as existing within yourself?" I asked.

"What? Nothing! There is nothing about her that I see in myself," Sunny responded.

"Sunny, there is a human-potential concept called 'the mirror.' It is used in many trainings and some mental health counselors even use it as the basis of their practice. The mirror can be approached in several ways: 1. That which you resist and react to strongly in others is sure to be found within yourself; 2. That which you resist and react to in others is something you are afraid exists within yourself; 3. That which you resist in yourself, you will dislike in others."

"It certainly doesn't apply in my case," Sunny said sarcastically.

"Maybe not, Sunny, but let's look for reflections anyway. What quality do you dislike most in this woman you work with?"

"She's deceitful. Last week she took a research report out of my desk, read it, then discussed it with our boss before I even presented it to him. When I did, it was anticlimactic because he was already aware of the information."

"Okay. How are you deceitful in your life, Sunny, and with whom?"

"I don't think I am deceitful," she replied. "I hate deceit."

"I realize that, otherwise you wouldn't react so strongly. And it's time to be straight, Sunny. How are you deceitful and with whom?"

She scowled at me, looking directly into my eyes. I stared back just as directly. "I guess I have been deceitful with my boyfriend the last couple of months. I'm kind of in a quandary because I met someone else at work and I really like him. We have lunch together almost every day. I went out with him once while John was fishing with his friends. Are you saying that because I'm having a hard time with myself over that, I'm having a hard time with Mary at work?"

"I don't know, Sunny. Is that it?"

She didn't respond.

"There's one more aspect to the mirror concept, and that is, you become what you resist."

Sunny sat down, rubbing her neck even harder.

3.
Your Earthly Purpose

*Adapted From A Seminar Talk by Dick Sutphen in
Fort Lauderdale, Florida, March 1987.*

"How many of you would like to know why you are
here on earth, and what your purpose is in living your
current life?"

(Most of the hands in the audience are raised.)

"All right, God told me to tell you!"

(Laughter)

"Don't laugh, **she** did! She wants you to know that
you're here to raise your vibrational rate by resolving
your karma and fulfilling your dharma. And you're going
to do this by letting go of fear and learning to express
unconditional love.

"To let go of fear means to rise above fear-based emotions, such as anger, selfishness, jealousy, hate, repression, envy, greed, possessiveness, anxiety, guilt,
insecurity, inhibitions, egoism, vanity, malice, and resentment. Fear is a very big word.

"When I say unconditional love, I'm not talking about
romantic love. Unconditional love means not limited by

21

conditions—it is the acceptance of others without judgment, without blame or expectations. It is accepting others as they are without attempting to change them, except through your own positive example.

"But let's begin at the beginning. How many of you in this room accept that you are spiritual beings?"

(All hands appear to be raised.)

"All right, we all seem to be in agreement on that. Then wouldn't it follow that in reality you are already a highly evolved, enlightened soul? But lifetimes of experiences have created so much subconscious fear programming, you no longer realize who you really are. You've trapped yourself on the wheel of reincarnation until you resolve these fears because they are the lessons you must learn in order to attain the freedom you desire.

"To better explain this, I want to share some information about science and metaphysics. First, the entire universe operates on the same principal of **vibrational energy.** And **you are vibrational energy.** You were born into this life with a vibrational rate you earned in the past. Everyone in this room has a different vibrational rate, and whether you realize it or not, your purpose is to raise it.

"As an example, let's assume that vibrational rates vary from zero to 1,000. And for the sake of this discussion, let's accept that the metaphysical teachers are correct, and there are seven levels on the other side in the non-physical realms of spirit. The lower astral planes would be the lowest vibrational level and a very undesirable place to be. And the seventh, or Godhead level, would be the highest, or 1,000.

"We'll pretend that you were born with a rate of 400. This is the rate you've earned as a result of how you lived your past lives, and from your efforts while in spirit between lifetimes. How you live your current life will

ERRATUM

On page 23, 1st paragraph, copy should read:

"If you rise above some of your fears, pass some of your karmic tests and live a basically positive life, you'll probably raise your rate. But if you live a life filled with negativity (anger, hostility, resentment, etc.), you'll probably lower your rate. I'm sure Hitler lowered his vibrational rate just about as low as it could go.

determine if you will raise or lower your vibrational rate.

"If you rise above some of your fears, pass some of your karmic tests and live a basically positive life, you'll probably lower your rate. I'm sure Hitler lowered his vibrational rate just about as low as it could go.

"Let's assume you live a positive life and raise your vibrational rate from 400 to 465. The rate of 400 might have placed you on the third level in spirit. But 465 might place you on the fourth level. So, when you die and cross over, you'll find yourself drawn to the fourth level. You could go back down and visit the lower vibration of the third level, but because it is less desirable than the fourth level, you would not remain there. You might visit the fifth level, which is more desirable than the fourth, but you would be unable to tolerate the more intense vibrations of the fifth level for long.

"Why do you want to raise your vibrational rate? Maybe it is because you want to get up to the seventh level. Or, it could be the only way to get off the wheel of reincarnation. That's a pretty good reason. Or, maybe this is how we procreate additional energy for an energy gestalt that we are part of. Within your Higher-Self is what Carl Jung calls the "collective unconscious." Metaphysics teaches us that we are all one, and since we are all part of the collective unconscious, this is correct. We are all connected on this level. Maybe we are all part of a great energy gestalt called 'God.' If so, then since we are part of God, we **are** God. And we are dedicated to doing our part to increase the energy of the whole.

"Are you following me this far?" (Enthusiastic response from the audience.) "Okay, let's put what is known scientifically about vibrational energy into the context of your life.

"Albert Einstein discovered that **matter is energy.** Matter appears solid but is, in reality, pulsating molecules

23

of energy. That chair you are sitting on appears solid, but it is composed of zillions of pulsating molecules of energy. The molecules are vibrating at a specific rate and are held together by the yin/yang tension of the earth plane.

"So, your chair is energy, and that plant over in the corner of the room is energy. Your body is energy. Your mind is energy. Your soul is energy. And the only difference between the chair and plant and your body, mind and soul is their vibrational rate. Your highest vibrational rate will exist in your Higher-Self, or God-Self—the superconscious level of your mind. The level of the collective unconscious.

"But let's continue to explore what we know scientifically about energy. The physicists have isolated the smallest molecule of energy within a sealed cloud chamber. Nothing else can get in and nothing can get out. The molecule is far too small to see with the naked eye, but it can be photographed on ultra-high sensitive film.

"The film shows that the molecule has a size, a weight, a pattern, and a speed. And it exists within the cloud chamber until it finally falls to the bottom, appearing to die. But it doesn't die. The scientists leave the camera on, and pretty soon, the molecule is back. It has transformed: It has a new size, a new weight, a new pattern, and a new speed. And this goes on indefinitely.

"Energy can't die—it can only transform. **And you are energy! You can't die, you can only transform. How do you transform? You reincarnate.** You reincarnate because you can raise your vibrational rate faster on the manifest plane than you can in spirit. And maybe you desire to move on up to a more desirable level on the other side. And maybe the goal of our entire energy gestalt is to generate more energy, because **energy can't stand still.** It must, by its very nature, move forward or backward. To stand still is to stagnate.

"And you are energy, so the same is true of you, as an individual part of the energy gestalt. You are either moving forward or backward, preparing to transform. Do you know what makes your energy move forward?" (Dick pauses and stares at the audience.)

"Aliveness! Aliveness causes your energy to move forward, creating more energy. Aliveness is real enjoyment in doing what you do. It is excitement, exhilaration that makes you feel glad to be alive! It's the joy, stimulation and pleasure that make life worth living. And it is the expression of unconditional love.

"Aliveness is critical to your mental, physical and spiritual well-being. But, for many people, life is pretty long on misery and short on joy and aliveness. You repress who you really are by wearing masks and hiding your real feelings. You become so concerned with what other people think that you lose your own identity. You accept the expectations of others and succumb to your fears.

"When you succumb to your fears, you keep invalid beliefs, you give away your freedom, and you begin to close down and burn out. And life becomes routine, dull and boring. But your mind can't handle 'boring,' so you create places to hide ... like sitting in front of the TV set, or indulging in gossip, or maybe you hide in excess sleep, escapist reading, or metaphysical 'cosmic foo-foo.' There are many places to hide.

"But if the places you create to hide are as empty as those I just described, you'll still be bored, so your mind will have to create something to make life more interesting. The brain/mind researchers have proven that your mind can't accept a mundane existence for long.

"Maybe fighting with your mate would make life more interesting. At least when you hurt, you know you're alive. Or your mind could create a health problem. Kidney stones would give you something to talk about, wouldn't it? Or how about an accident? If your life is endangered, you'd experience a lot of aliveness.

"Your mind is vibrational energy, which must move forward or backward. Boredom is stagnation—energy moving backward and preparing to transform. If you want to live and drive your energy forward, you'd better make your life interesting on your own, or your mind will do it for you.

"I suggest you incorporate more positive challenge into your life. Challenge is critical to your well-being. As a natural expression of energy, when there is no longer any challenge, transformation follows. You can observe this in people or nations. History proves every nation that has reached its peak has fragmented and collapsed when unopposed or no longer challenged by other nations.

"I've observed couples who have struggled through all kinds of adversity until they finally resolved their difficulties and accomplished their goals. When there was no longer any challenge, they got a divorce. I've known very spiritual people who have attained the enlightenment they sought for so long only to backslide and have to start over again with a new challenge. To keep your energy moving forward, you need aliveness and challenge in all areas of your life.

"This is even true of spiritual evolution. **Challenge is very spiritual!** But most metaphysical people don't realize this. Other New Age teachers have argued with me. They claim meditation is the path to enlightenment. They are wrong, and today, with our awareness of brain/mind technology, it is easy to explain the fallacy of their ideas.

"Meditation assists you in detaching from the stress and anxiety of the manifest world. And there is no doubt that it is very effective in this area. The problem is, the detachment is right across the board. You will detach from all the positive aspects of your life as well. The same thing

26

happens when you take valium or smoke grass. Meditation is healthier, but it won't work as a spiritual path if used to excess.

"There is nothing wrong with a short daily meditation session, but if you do it for 40 minutes every morning and evening as some people do, you will constantly remain in an alpha level of consciousness. This can be easily demonstrated with an EEG machine.

"No wonder the gurus who want you to join their organizations encourage meditation. The more you meditate, the mellower you become, until your mind begins to go 'flat.' And the more you meditate, the more you detach from reality and become willing to respond to command. You've seen the groups in white robes, shaved heads and blank eyes on the street corners. Their organization keeps them meditating and chanting several hours a day.

"I contend we are here on earth to learn to consciously detach from negativity, while we are wide awake in full beta consciousness, not stoned. And until we can go through an entire lifetime with total involvement in life, without fear, we will continue to reincarnate upon the earth.

"So the idea is to generate a lot of aliveness and challenge in your life and use the resulting opportunities to rise above the fears, expressing unconditional love. It is how you'll raise your vibrational rate and spiritually evolve. And it is also how you'll keep yourself mentally and physically healthy.

"The brain/mind researchers are proving again and again with their research that positive people with exciting lives are sick far less than others. And anyone can create a positive, exciting life. It doesn't take money, but it does take some effort. You have to decide exactly what you want and then do something about it.

"And maybe the best place to begin is with a quick exploration of aliveness in your life. Let's do a short process in which I'll ask you some yes and no questions and you decide for yourself if there are areas that need changing."

(At this time in the seminar, Dick induced a group altered state of consciousness, using large-screen video projection. In an altered state, the filters that normally inhibit the subconscious and superconscious mind are removed, and an individual's attention focuses only upon one thing—the input received in response to the questions or directions of the hypnotist. Once the group was ready, Dick proceeded to ask them many questions about each area of their life. Each individual was encouraged to decide if they needed to create additional aliveness, and how to attain the goal.)

*You and you alone
have erected
the barrier
between yourself
and liberation.*

4.

How To End Suffering
And Attain Peace Of Mind

*Spiritual-potential principles from the book
"Enlightenment Transcripts."*

If you want to end suffering and attain peace of mind, your only help is **self-help!** Unless you need hospital treatment or prescription drugs, all that gurus, religions or mental health counselors can do to help you is: **1.** alter your viewpoint, or **2.** make you aware of your unconscious programming. **The rest is up to you.**

This section offers four concepts that will allow you to end suffering and attain peace of mind. That may sound presumptuous, but that's what is. The concepts are the answer. It's quite simple, but that doesn't mean it's easy. It takes time to become fully aware of the wisdom which can erase your disharmonious karma. It also takes time and self-discipline to incorporate this awareness into your life. But when you do, it will serve as the foundation from which you'll express unconditional love.

To be a **Master of Life** in today's society means to be self-actualized and aware in a very unaware world that

29

wants you to fit its mold and accept its ideas. These teachings offer a philosophy/religion of self that you don't join ... you live. The awareness is the soul of spirituality and is based upon Zen, metaphysics, logic, contemporary therapy, and brain/mind research.

1.
Karma & Reincarnation
Accept karma as your philosophical basis of reality. In so doing, you accept total self-responsibility.

Reincarnation was taught by Buddha, Krishna and Rama, and is part of all the great Eastern religions. It is also taught by contemporary metaphysical organizations, and as you are probably already aware, these great teachers, religions and groups don't agree on much except the concept of reincarnation. Reincarnation was taught by the Essenes, with whom Jesus had considerable contact. The historian Josephus refers to reincarnation as a common belief among Jews at the time of Jesus.

Several references to reincarnation appear to remain in the Christian Bible, although most were deleted. Some of the Old Testament books were compiled no earlier than the seventh and eighth centuries B.C. Jesus' teachings were not written down in his lifetime but were handed down verbally from disciple to disciple. Most of the New Testament was written in the second and third centuries A.D.

In tracing the origin of the Bible, one is led to A.D. 325, when Constantine the Great called the First Council of Nicaea, composed of 300 religious leaders. Three centuries after Jesus lived, this council was given the task of separating divinely inspired writings from those of questionable origin.

The actual compilation of the Bible was an incredibly

complicated project that involved churchmen of many varying beliefs, in an atmosphere of dissension, jealousy, intolerance, persecution, and bigotry.

At this time, the question of the divinity of Jesus had split the church into two factions. Constantine offered to make the little-known Christian sect the official state religion if the Christians would settle their differences. Apparently, he didn't particularly care what they believed in as long as they agreed upon a belief. By compiling a book of sacred writings, Constantine thought that the book would give authority to the new church. It is a matter of historical record that only after much hostility and bitterness at the Council of Nicaea was Jesus declared to be the "Essence of the Father."

The fact that reincarnation had at one time been in the Bible is indisputable, for in A.D. 533, during the Second Council of Constantinople, the church adopted a decree stating:

> Whosoever shall support the mythical doctrine of the pre-existence of the soul and the subsequent wonderful opinion of its return, let him be anathema.

Nothing can be canceled by official decree unless its existence is being acknowledged in the first place! Reincarnation was probably removed because the church leaders thought it let people be independent by allowing them self-responsibility for their own actions and the opportunity to balance karma in future lives. These leaders decided it was better to tell people, "There is only one life. If you don't live the way we tell you is the right way to live, you'll go to hell." That made it much easier to control the masses.

So, if you accept that reincarnation was once also part of Christianity, then it becomes the core belief of almost all spirituality in the world. And the system that makes reincarnation workable and logical is **karma.**

It is easy to say you accept karma, but I've found that most people do not fully comprehend what it means.

It is easy to explain karma in one sentence: If you act positively, you'll experience harmony, and if you act negatively, you'll experience disharmony. The word karma means action. And there are three kinds of action:

1. Mental action
2. Verbal action
3. Physical action

From a karmic viewpoint, the effect of your actions are harmonious, disharmonious or neutral. Karma is personal and collective. The world we are currently experiencing has been formed by our collective karma.

If you want to know about your past karma, simply look at your current state of mind, your body, your success or lack of success, your relationships ... or lack of them. If you want to know what will happen in the future, look at what your mind concentrates on now. On a regular basis, what do you think about? Pettiness, gossip, small talk, negativity? Or do you dwell upon positive things, loving emotions, compassion, and service?

You are creating your own future right now, and you can view this from the perspective of cause and effect in the context of your present life. Everything you've ever experienced is recorded in the memory banks of your subconscious mind. According to brain researchers, your subconscious mind has 200,000 times the capacity of the largest computer ever built, so recording your entire past isn't too great a task. These past experiences represent all your programming and it is your programming that has made you what you are today. Your talents and abilities, problems, and afflictions are the result of your past programming, which is your karma.

You create your own reality, or karma, as a response to

everything you **think, say** and **do.** But to begin with, you must understand that **karma either is or it isn't.** It is not a halfway proposition. This is either a random universe or there is meaning to life.

The nihilistic viewpoint is that we came from nowhere—we just appeared—and when we die, we become nothing ... no reason, no plan, no point to our existence. Life is totally meaningless. Or there is a plan behind existence. If there is a plan, then an intelligence must be behind the plan. You can call the intelligence by any name you desire: God, universal mind, energy gestalt, collective unconscious, to name a few.

And if there is a plan, it follows that justice must be part of it. Justice! But look around you. Where is there justification for misery and inequality? How can you justify child abuse, mass starvation, rapes, murders, wars, victims of violence, people ripping off other people and seemingly being rewarded for it?

Karma can explain it all! I've studied philosophy and religion all my life and nothing else can logically explain the inequality. Karma rewards and punishes. It is a multi-life debit and credit system that offers total justice. But what we can't forget is that karma either is or it isn't. There can be no halfway plan, no halfway justice. Either absolutely everything is karmic or nothing is karmic. You need to accept or reject the concept of karma; it is senseless and confusing to accept a halfway position.

Now, to bring some of this awareness together: If I pick up a stone and toss it into a pond, I am the cause and the effect is the splash and ripples. I have disturbed the harmony of the pond. The ripples flow out and back until, due to the physical law of dissipation of energy, the pond eventually returns to its original harmonious state.

And, like the rock, everything negative that you think, say, or do creates vibrations that flow out and back until eventually, through your lifetimes, you balance your karma ... until your own harmony is restored. Everything you **think, say** and **do** creates or erases karma. And, if that's not enough to deal with, this includes the **motive, intent** and **desire** behind every thought and action.

When you begin to explore the motive, intent and desire behind everything you think, say and do, you'll find you're asking yourself a lot of questions. Are you helping your friend out of true compassion or because it pumps up your ego? Or because your friend is now in debt to you? Do you give to charity at the office because you desire to help, or because you are afraid of what people in the office will think if you don't. It's easy to appear to be creating harmonious karma when you really aren't, because of your motive, intent or desire. **Why** you do what you do is just as important as **what** you do from a karmic perspective.

I also contend that neither God nor the Lords of Karma bestow your suffering upon you. It is **your** decision and **yours alone** to tackle the opportunities you are experiencing in your life. Only you are responsible for absolutely everything that has ever happened to you. You are your own judge and jury. In your Higher Mind, you are fully aware that in order to progress, you must learn. And the fastest way to learn is by directly experiencing the actual consequences of your own actions.

And, if you and you alone are responsible for absolutely everything that has ever happened to you, that means **everything!** This is very hard for some people to accept: There is no one to blame for **anything** that has ever happened to you. **There is no one to blame for anything!** The concept of blame is totally incompatible with karma. There are no victims. The ex-mate you had such a hard time with, the partner who ripped you off, the in-laws you hated, your sadistic boss, the guy who raped you when you were only 12, the burglars who robbed your house ... you created them all because you needed the self-punishment **or** you wanted to test yourself.

Take a moment and think back on your life. Think about everyone in your past who really made life difficult for you. In actuality, these were the people who helped you the most in accomplishing your goal of spiritual evolution. They helped you balance your karma. They were a test you created to determine how well you're progressing in attaining a perspective of unconditional love.

It is easy to tell whether you are passing or failing your own tests. If you respond with love, positive thoughts and compassion, you are probably passing the test. If you respond with negativity and blame, you are probably failing. And if you choose to fail, that is all right ... you'll just have to come back and try it again! If neither one learns this time, you will come back together in a future life for another opportunity. If one learns and the other doesn't, the one who learns has resolved the karma. The one who didn't will find someone else with a similar karmic configuration and they will come together to test themselves in the future.

Often in balancing karma, you don't even have to wait for the next lifetime for an opportunity to arise. We have all observed recurring, undesirable patterns in others, as well as in ourselves. This is a situation of learning through **pain** until we finally "get it," once and for all, that what we are doing doesn't work.

You were born with the package of karma that you desired to experience. From a spiritual perspective, if you are testing yourself, it is only your reactions to the experiences that are important.

When we are on the other side in spirit, preparing to enter into a lifetime, I sometimes think we go through a period of what I call being "very brave."

For instance, you may say to yourself, "Okay, I think I'm ready to test myself in another relationship with Donald. If he's willing, we'll fall in love, get married and have three children. When I'm about 32, Donald will begin to ignore me and start having affairs with other women. This time, because I owe Don one in this area, I'll emotionally support him and let him go with unconditional love."

As I said, you are "very brave" and aware over there on the other side. Now comes the reality. And what do you do? You scream and threaten and blame. You hire a lawyer who socks it to Donald financially for the rest of his days. You and Donald now hate each other. This is another example of learning through pain. You and Don can plan to return for another round in the year 2046; maybe the next time you will work it out.

Actually, there is no such thing as failing your own karmic test. If you fell off your bicycle nine times before you finally learned to ride, the nine failures were actually small successes which eventually led to the ultimate success. How many times you fail before reaching your goal is up to you.

In addition to your birth karma, you are creating new karma every day, both harmonious and disharmonious. And you are paying it off every day through the balancing effects of your subconscious mind.

There is also karma as yet unknown to you. It is stored up from the past, waiting for a suitable opportunity to discharge itself. This could happen later in this life or in your next life or in a lifetime after that. Not everything can be balanced in one lifetime.

But the good news is, the Law of Grace supersedes the Law of Karma. This means that if you give love, grace and mercy, you will receive it in return. All of your positive and loving thoughts and actions go to cancel your stored-up, bad karma. And since this is so, it is probably time for you to begin to think about how you can be more positive, loving and compassionate; how you can support good works and serve this planet ... if only to reduce the amount of undesirable karma that you have waiting for you in your future.

I also contend that **wisdom erases karma** and that we can mitigate karmic discomforts through awareness. The techniques of past-life therapy are often of value in this area. In the past, we've learned through pain. In other words, we've learned not to touch hot stoves because by touching hot stoves, we burn our fingers. After experiencing the pain of touching many hot stoves, we finally learn, once and for all, that it doesn't work to touch hot stoves. Of course, the hot stoves are the karmic lessons we need to learn in the areas of physical life, relationships, respect for life, greed, etc.

Instead, by learning through wisdom, we accept what we need to learn by becoming aware of the lesson, forgiving ourselves and letting go of it. Karma simply seeks to restore your disturbed equilibrium. You can do it the hard way through pain ... or the easy way through wisdom and grace.

Of course, to learn through wisdom, you must **forgive yourself.** Since you are your own judge and jury, it is up to you to forgive yourself. The only problem is that you will not do this unless you feel that the karma is totally balanced or that the lesson is learned. You can't fool yourself in this area. To truly forgive yourself, you must know, on every level of your body and mind, that you will never, ever forget the lesson again.

If you are not yet able to forgive yourself to this degree, you must decide what you can do to achieve this desired level of self-forgiveness. Can you do something symbolic to show that you have learned? Can you assist others as a form of restitution?

In working with people in past-life therapy, I've found that what I call "symbolic restitution" can be very powerful. As an example, I'll share the case of a man who suffered severe back problems for most of his adult life. Medically, nothing was found to be wrong with him. In regression, he relived a past life as a soldier in World War I. During battle, an artillery shell exploded near him, sending shrapnel into his back. He died slowly, in great pain, over a period of several days, feeling much bitterness toward the enemy.

With this knowledge revealed, he decided to become actively involved in the peace movement. This was a couple of years ago, and since then, he has strongly supported world peace organizations. And his back is slowly improving.

In another case, a woman with a long history of relationship problems relived a past life as a man who mistreated, raped and beat many women. As a form of symbolic restitution, the woman began volunteering her time to assist in a clinic for battered women. In this way, she will quickly attain, through wisdom, an awareness of the pain caused by such actions.

Self-Testing Karma

All karma can be categorized as self-reward or self-punishment. And, from a larger perspective, all karma is self-testing. This simply means that you create a situation to test yourself to see if you have learned your lessons on every level of your body and mind.

Self-testing could easily be combined with reward karma. Suppose you have earned the karmic right to easy wealth and fame. It is also a very important self-test to see if you can handle it correctly from a karmic perspective.

Do you use the money and position selfishly or do you use it as an opportunity to assist others? Often, the results of the test will indicate if you will allow yourself to retain the reward throughout your entire lifetime.

Another reward example might be a good marriage. Your test comes when the marriage hits a bumpy road. How do the two of you handle it? Let's say that you both respond with love. Chances are you'll remain together and not have to experience the more intense and long-range pain that would have resulted from the parting if you both hadn't learned your karmic lesson.

But let's explore it from another perspective. Let's assume that you are the female and you handle the problems with little or no compassion. You immediately leave your husband and take up with someone new. You have probably failed your own test. Now, let's say that the husband is very hurt, but he handles the parting with love and compassion and lets you go in a very supportive way. He may very well have passed his test, at the same time paying off old karma by being left. Maybe he left someone under similar circumstances in his last lifetime and he is balancing the situation.

The outcome wasn't predestined. You were both always capable of exercising your free will. Had you remained together, he may have had to wait until some future lifetime or event to balance the old debt. But since circumstances worked out the way they did, he resolved a karmic test and also karmic self-punishment in this one situation.

Self-Reward Karma

Reward karma is all the good stuff you've earned in the past. It could manifest in major aspects of life, such as easily attained wealth, a naturally healthy body or a good relationship with your mate. Or, reward karma could simply be viewed as the right to be born under more ideal astrological influences. We are all walking examples of our astrological birth times. While one set of planetary combinations may generate a mellow, self-confident personality, another combination may result in a hyperactive or self-destructive personality. Although all planetary configurations have both positive and negative aspects, some are more easily overcome than others.

Self-Punishment Karma

Self-punishment is exactly what it sounds like. You've done something disharmonious in the past and the quickest way to learn is to directly experience the consequences of your actions.

As an example, let's say you find yourself in a situation of extreme poverty to balance a past life in which you totally misused wealth. This is self-punishment. It is also self-testing, for your life is so miserable that it would be easy to turn to crime or to commit suicide. The test is to live through it properly.

The Five Categories of Karma

There are five categories of karma which fall either under self-reward or self-punishment.

Balancing Karma

This is the most simplistic, mechanical kind of cause and effect. Examples of balancing karma would be a lonely man who seeks unsuccessfully to establish a relationship. In a past life, he used others so cruelly that he needs to learn the value of a relationship.

Other examples: A man who is always overlooked for promotion because in a past life he destroyed others to attain wealth and power; a woman who suffers continual, severe migraine headaches because, in a fit of jealousy, she hit her lover on the head and killed him in a past incarnation; a man who is born blind because, as a Roman soldier, he purposely blinded Christian prisoners.

Physical Karma

Physical karma is a situation in which a past-life problem or misuse of the body results in an appropriate affliction in a later life.

As an example, a child born with lung problems might relate back to excessive smoking and death from lung cancer in a past life. Another man with a large, disfiguring birthmark found that it was a carry-over from a terrible burn in a past incarnation.

False-Fear Karma

False-fear karma is created when a traumatic past-life incident generates a fear that is not valid in the context of the current life.

For example, a workaholic finds out in regression that he couldn't feed his family during a time of famine in the Middle Ages. He re-experiences the pain of burying a child who starved to death. In his current life, his subconscious mind is attempting to avert any potential duplication of that terrible mental pain, thus generating an internal drive to work day and night and assure that he adequately provides for his family in this incarnation.

False-fear karma and guilt karma are the easiest to resolve through past-life therapy techniques because once the individuals understand the origin of the fear and/or guilt, they can see how it no longer applies to them in their current lifetime.

False-Guilt Karma

False-guilt karma occurs when an individual takes on the responsibility or accepts the blame for a traumatic past-life incident for which he or she is blameless from any perspective.

A man who contracted polio resulting in a paralyzed leg perceived as the past-life cause his being the driver of a car which was involved in an accident that crippled a child. Although it wasn't his fault, he blames himself and seeks self-forgiveness through this karmic affliction.

In another situation, a young woman with terrible physical and emotional problems regressed to a past-life in which a violent and unstable soldier was attracted to her. She was repulsed by him and did not respond to his courting. As a warning to her if she continued to refuse him, he cut off the hands of her best friend. The woman felt responsibility and guilt over the loss of her friend's hands, and in an attempt to pay a debt she didn't owe, she created a traumatic life for herself.

Situations involving depression and/or emotional problems combined with physical problems can almost always be traced to a tragedy of some kind in which **guilt** is associated with the event. This can be false guilt or a situation in which the troubled individual was actually responsible for the tragedy.

Developed Ability and Awareness Karma

Abilities and awareness are developed over a period of many lifetimes.

A man in Rome became interested in music and began to develop his ability. Today, after six additional lifetimes in which he became a little better with each life, he is a successful professional musician.

As another example, a woman who has been happily married for 35 years has worked hard to refine her awareness of human relationships over many lifetimes.

The abilities and awareness that you master over a period of lifetimes are yours to keep forever, although they may lie latent, buried deep within you, waiting for a time when it seems appropriate to call them into your present existence.

Destiny Versus Free Will

In becoming aware of karma, some people begin to feel helpless, as if everything were predestined. This is not how it works. Some things are destined when you come into a life. These are usually major life areas, and you are born with astrological configurations that dictate how you are going to approach your life opportunities. But, as you live your life, moving toward the predestined events, you can mitigate circumstances and exercise free will in your response to everything you experience. It may even be possible to live your life in such a way as to cancel the need for learning in a particular area. Wisdom erases karma, and in changing how you think, act and react, you change your future.

2.
What Is, Is

The second step to assist you to end suffering and attain peace of mind is to accept that what is, is. As simple as this concept is, I've been studying it for years and I still continue to learn more about it. Life on earth includes suffering. That's pretty obvious. We have relationship problems, we lose loved ones through separation or death, we experience loneliness, sickness and accidents. We are haunted by guilt. We have monetary hardships, experience phobias and fears, and have unfulfilled desires.

We experience this distress because we desire things to be different than they are. In short, it is your resistance to what is that causes your suffering. And when I say suffering, I mean everything in your life that doesn't work. Do you want to see an immediate, positive change in your life? Then stop resisting what is. Some things are facts. Income taxes exist ... that's what is. Gravity exists ... that's what is. Your mate is quiet and stubborn ... that's what is. You can spend your life attempting to change what is, but there isn't much you're going to do about it. Instead, concentrate your efforts upon that which you can change.

A short Christian prayer says the same thing: "God grant me the serenity to accept the things I cannot change, the courage to change the things I can, and the wisdom to know the difference."

But you should hear the resistance to this concept that I receive in seminars. People want things changed. In fact, they want everything they dislike changed, and initially, they think I am advocating total, passive acceptance of life as it is. That is not the case.

Maybe the powers that be have decided to build a maximum security prison a few blocks from your house. That is not necessarily what is. You have the power to gather your neighbors and petition the state to build it elsewhere. There are things you have the potential to change, so do everything you can to change them if it is important to you. But there are also things you cannot change and I advocate that you recognize these areas of your life and stop wasting your efforts attempting to change what cannot be changed.

When you begin to accept what is in your life, you simply accept facts, logic ... unalterable realities. Actually, you have no choice in accepting what is. It is what is. But you certainly have a choice in how you respond to what is. You can handle it or make it worse by generating negative subconscious programming.

The wisdom of many of the old Zen Masters has been translated and is available for study today. My favorite Zen Master was Joshu, and Zen expressed through Joshu is radical, extreme and sometimes even brutal. He was born in China in A.D.778 and is believed to have died in A.D. 897 at the age of 120. My favorite Joshu story relates to his death. His students gathered around their dying master, and one asked, "Oh, Master, don't leave us without telling us the meaning of life." In response to this request, Joshu said, "What's hot is hot and what's cold is

44

cold!" And he died. It was his way of saying, what is, is.

3.
Conscious Detachment

There is **attached** mind and **detached** mind. The vast majority of people on this planet live out their lives knowing only attached mind. This means your state of mind is always changing from positive to negative as outside conditions change. This is extreme fluctuation from happiness and joy through **neutral** to the basement of emotions: depression, anger, hostility and other fears.

Here are some examples of attached mind: **1.** You are having a great day at the office until a co-worker makes a snide remark about your hair. Your response is inner anger and you dwell upon the situation for the rest of the day. **2.** You climbed into the shower with your brand-new electronic watch on. The water ruins it and you become depressed. **3.** You give a presentation at your club and it is well received. But afterward, someone whose opinion you respect criticizes your presentation and you respond with hostility.

The goal is to develop **detached** mind. This means your state of mind fluctuates only from positive to neutral as outside conditions change. You accept all the warmth and joy and happiness that life has to offer while detaching from negativity by allowing it to flow through you without affecting you. In other words, your state of mind drops no further than neutral.

Here are some examples of detached mind: **1.** You are having a great day at the office. When a co-worker makes a snide remark about your hair, your response is to let the remark flow through you without affecting you. You know the remark says a lot more about her than it does about your hair. **2.** You climb into the shower with your brand-new electronic watch on and the water ruins it. In

45

understanding that you can do nothing about it, you accept what is. You refuse to get upset and make matters worse by programming your subconscious mind with negativity. **3.** You give a presentation at your club and it is well received by all but one person, whose opinion you respect. When he criticizes your presentation, you respond, "Thank you for your opinion; that's what you got out of it." You are unaffected by the remark. You know your critic is speaking from his viewpoint which has nothing to do with the facts. You know your talk was well received and you've detached from the need to be right.

To develop conscious detachment means to detach only from the negativity in your life. It does not mean having no feelings or sensations such as hunger or pain. It is not artificial detachment based upon alpha level programming. It is detachment based upon conscious awareness of the logic of letting go and refusing to make matters worse than they already are.

I am not talking about psychological dissociation, which is a defense mechanism to avoid reality. I am not talking about repressing your natural negative emotions. As long as you feel the anger, hostility and resentment, you'll have to express it, or it will come out in another way.

But as you consciously come to realize when you are resisting what is and when you are making matters worse, you will start to back off due to **wisdom,** not repression. Be totally involved in your life and enjoy everything there is to enjoy while detaching from the negativity. When you eliminate the negativity, you leave more time and room for love and warm interaction. When you cease to be concerned about negativity, you'll be more likely to enter into what you do in life with nothing held back—free to be entirely at one with circumstance.

Until you can go through a lifetime of total involvement without generating disharmonious karma, you'll be tied

46

to the "cyclical existence of reincarnation." Another way to phrase that would be to say, until you can go through a lifetime of total involvement, only expressing unconditional love, you'll be tied to the cyclical existence of reincarnation. This is simply the bottom line on spiritual evolution.

4.
Viewpoint

Reality exists as that which you experience and the way you experience life is based solely upon the way you choose to view what happens to you. Your viewpoint is the deciding factor in whether you perceive life as a hostile experience or a tranquil oneness.

What you would call a negative situation in your life is only a problem if you look upon it as a problem. We all have the ability to transform the way we experience our lives, or in other words, change our perspective. As difficult as it may be to accept, our problems actually contribute satisfaction to our lives. If there were no problems to challenge you, there could be no growth. There would be no way for you to learn how to handle things and become aware of your capability for making your life work.

In fact, if you didn't have problems, you'd have to invent some to give yourself the opportunity to grow and learn and make your life work. And obviously, that is often what we do. We manifest problems, not consciously, but subconsciously we create these challenges.

The real secret to growth through problems is to look upon problems as opportunities. The bigger the problem, the bigger the opportunity. And the problem usually stays with us just as long as we need it to achieve an understanding of ourselves and others. Once we have that understanding, we can let go of the effect.

47

In many problem situations, nothing about the situation will change but our viewpoint. And yet, by changing our reaction to the situation, we eliminate the problem: we cease to resist it. Things may be at their worst and we remain happy. Each time we rise above a painful situation, we have attained soul growth. Hopefully, this awareness will make future problem situations of the same kind unnecessary.

What other people do
     does
     not
     affect
     you

What you think
     about
     what
     they
     do
     affects you.

From the book
KNOW THY HIGHER-SELF—1972
(out of print)

5.

The Basics Of Spirituality

Excerpt from "Past-Life Therapy In Action,"
co-written with Lauren Leigh Taylor.

Everyone has a subconscious desire to evolve to the level of a Master: a fully self-actualized individual who has risen above the need of earthly incarnations. Yet people with a reincarnation orientation often get side-tracked by concentrating on the esoteric aspects of their spiritual quest and forgetting about the basics. This tends to retard their spiritual advancement. The following are what I consider to be the basics:

* * *

A Master detaches from his illusions about reality and recognizes that it exists only as that which he experiences. It can be experienced as a hostile separateness or a tranquil oneness.

* * *

A Master accepts others as they are without attempting to change them to be what he wants them to be.

* * *

A Master is a living example of "detached mind." His state of mind fluctuates only from positive to neutral as outside conditions change. He accepts all the warmth and joy in life while detaching from the negativity by allowing it to flow past him without affecting him.

* * *

A Master doesn't complain to others about anyone or anything. He accepts "what is." He accepts unalterable realities as they are without wasting mental or physical energy attempting to change what cannot be changed.

* * *

A Master does not judge other human beings. He knows that everyone is doing the best they can, although maybe not the best they know how.

* * *

A Master doesn't blame anyone for anything. Blame is incompatible with the acceptance of karma. You and you alone are responsible for absolutely everything that has ever happened to you. You set it up to experience as an opportunity to learn.

* * *

A Master doesn't take anything personally, for he knows someone else's reaction to him, good or bad, comes out of their memory banks. It is their viewpoint and has nothing to do with him. The way they relate to him they would relate to anyone who represented to them what he represents.

* * *

A Master knows that there is nothing to seek and nothing to find. You are already enlightened, and all the words in the world will not give you what you already have. The wise seeker, therefore, is concerned with one thing only: to become aware of what he already is, of the True Self within.

6.

The Cause Of The Cause Of The Problem

From an article in MASTER OF LIFE magazine.

Everyone attending the **Reincarnation Intensive** five-day seminar in February 1987 was searching for answers. Many sought to resolve specific problems. The following are from the participants' Pre-Seminar Information Sheets: "I'm here to find out why I have constant anxiety, which produces psychosomatic disorders." "I want to learn more about my relationship with my husband and children, and why we play the games we do." "I need to find out why I can't seem to have a relationship with a man that lasts longer than three years."

"I have a wanderlust feeling that doesn't coincide with my spouse's desire to establish roots." "Why do I block receiving money and abundance and a mate?" "I need to be able to relate to my negative mother. I am uncomfortable around her and I resent her." "Why do I continue to attract relationships that are doomed to fail?" "I need to know about the karma between my son and myself." "Why, with the whole world open to me now, do I seem to have no passions and no goals?"

The seminar was devoted to exploring many aspects of reincarnation. On the fourth day, Dick conducted an extra-intensive "Back To The Cause" regression which included many questions about resolving the fear associated with the problem, and how to more rapidly resolve the karma, if possible.

The following are just a few of the participants' reactions during the post-session sharing, along with an in-depth examination of Dorothy's problems and an individual regression to her childhood in this life, then back to a previous incarnation.

Simon

Simon: "I asked, 'Why do I create such guilt and self-punishment?' And the pertinent lifetime 'lit up' almost before we had even gotten started. I was a female prostitute. And I was raped by some soldiers. Afterward, I became a prostitute for money. Maybe this explains why money is such a big deal for me today. I don't like money. I don't want to have it. In the regression, I realized that every time I got money, I was trading it for the use of my body ... for my body to be abused. But I became very wealthy in that lifetime. Obviously, I was very good at what I did." (laughter) "But I hated myself for it. I evidently played the game ... that I was supposed to be proud of myself, look at all the money and material rewards I obtained. Society accepted me because I had a lot of money. I was living a lie and hating myself for it."

Donna

Donna: "I've always had an irrational fear that when I have a baby, somehow the baby will smother in its sleep or choke in another room while taking its nap. Or that a child would be physically hurt. I always thought it was normal—just the usual pre-parent worries about kids.

But today, I thought I'd explore it further and go back to the cause of this fear.

"I saw myself in a medieval setting, in an old stone house with arches. There was a baby in a cradle by a window. And I was going to the cradle, and the baby was very white, very still and very cold. And then I picked it up and it was dead. Then a man came into the room ... my husband, I think. He said, 'These things happen, you have to realize this. There was nothing you could have done.'

"When you asked about how to resolve the fear, I got that I need to stop being so worried and crazy. My present emotions are being programmed by the past, but in reality have nothing to do with the present."

Larry

Larry: "Most of this lifetime, I have resented authority and power. I refuse to place myself in any kind of an authority position. And in the regression, I went back to Egypt, 580 B.C. I was a person of great authority. My wife and two children were very resentful about what was happening in the country at that time, and they openly expressed their hostility. Eventually, I was forced to execute them. In time, I was myself tortured and executed.

"An important revelation of the regression is that my children from that life are my parents in this life." [*Note: The day before, Larry had related another regression to his negative relationship with his parents.*]

"And what I've been doing in my present life is going around and looking for punishment. And anyone who has authority or power ... well, I feel like they are going to punish me." (sobbing)

"I don't know what I'm going to do about it yet. When you asked about 'symbolic restitution,' I got that I was to continue to work with people, and help them in whatever way I can ... to explore themselves."

53

Dorothy

Dorothy: "I'm feeling very frustrated." (choking with emotion) "Yesterday, I didn't get very good impressions. Today, when I got out of the tunnel, I was bare-footed, and there was a little girl, and she was very, very frightened." (crying, heavy sobbing) "I don't know why. I know why it might relate to this lifetime, but I don't know if the regressive impressions were from this life or a past life. And that's all I got ... and I just got into that fear and I couldn't get out of it. I'm still in it."

Dick: "You've been avoiding it until now, Dorothy. Now you are getting close. My regression instructions were phrased, 'I am going to direct you back into your past. You may go back to an earlier time in your present life, or you may return to an event that transpired in a previous incarnation.' So you may have been recalling a childhood incident in this life. On your pre-seminar information sheet was the question, 'What would you most like to learn about yourself in this seminar?' And you answered, 'Why I chose my parents, who gave me to an older couple when I was 2½ years old, and why I chose them to parent me.'"

Dorothy: "Yes, I know all the things that happened in this lifetime. I had reason to be afraid. And I think I have forgiven my mother and my father and everyone concerned. And I don't know why I'm still so afraid."

Dick: "I'd like to do another regression. Are you willing to be individually regressed so we can explore this in more detail?"

Dorothy: "Yes."

[Note: Dorothy leans back in a recliner lounge in the front of the room and the lights are dimmed.]

Dick: "All right, before we begin the regression, I want to talk to you, Dorothy. Do you feel that your fearful experience was related to your childhood experiences in

54

this life?"

Dorothy: "Yes, but all I sensed was extreme fear of being abandoned." (sobs) "And rejected and left all alone. I was abandoned as a child, but I wasn't left alone. I was left with foster parents."

Dick: "How has that experience affected your life as an adult?"

Dorothy: "Well, I've felt alone and lonely quite a bit as an adult. The man I was married to was a workaholic. When we first got married, he went to school; he was either at school or he was studying, but he didn't have much time for me. Then, when he was out of school, he worked long hours, so he not only didn't have time for me, he was almost never home."

Dick: "Did you feel abandoned by him?"

Dorothy: "Yes, I felt abandoned and unloved. And, although I asked for the divorce, I ended up feeling rejected by him—he didn't really try to get me back. He didn't fight the divorce."

Dick: "Is that why you filed for the divorce, to see if he cared?"

Dorothy: "That wasn't what I was thinking of. I just felt it was a dishonest marriage. On the surface, everything looked good. We had a nice home and two fine sons, we got along pretty well and everything seemed fine. But I felt it was dishonest because we didn't really have an intimate relationship as far as being able to talk to one another. It was all superficial. And I just couldn't live with that any more."

Dick: "Did you really talk to your husband, Dorothy? Did you share from your heart, unreservedly?"

Dorothy: "I couldn't really tell him what I was feeling! No, I didn't."

Dick: "So you weren't communicating with him any more than he was with you?"

Dorothy: "No! It was as much my fault as his, I realize that."

Dick: "Did you feel if you left him and found someone else that you would be able to just immediately communicate with that person?"

Dorothy: "Yes, that's exactly what I thought."

Dick: "What happened?"

Dorothy: "Well, I haven't had a lot of relationships. Actually, there was only one really close relationship since then. I was able to talk to that man quite a bit, but there were some major disagreements between us. He wanted to get married, and I wasn't ready to get married, so he found someone else. Then I felt rejected, even though he had asked me to marry him and I declined. I still felt rejected."

Dick: "So we have a pattern emerging. Is there any other time in your life that you recall having felt rejected under similar circumstances?"

Dorothy: "There were a couple of other men I felt rejected by, but I wasn't that interested in them."

Dick: "Did you test them, Dorothy? Did you set it up for rejection to see how much they cared?"

Dorothy: "Ah, well . . . the last man who rejected me . . . I don't know. I guess I set that up. I knew when I started seeing him that he wasn't really my type."

Dick: "So the outcome was assured?"

Dorothy: "Yes."

Dick: "What would a man have to do to prove that he really loved you? Or do you think that you could even allow that?"

Dorothy: (long pause) "Well, he wouldn't have to do anything special. Just be himself. . . ."

Dick: "Just be himself and love you in exactly the way you want him to love you?"

Dorothy: "And also allow me to be myself."

Dick: "Didn't your husband allow you to be yourself?"

Dorothy: "No, he was a Baptist and set in his ways. He was extremely self-righteous. His constant moralizing made me feel I was bad. He was very unaccepting of me."

Dick: "Okay, Dorothy, let's condense your primary problem before we begin to explore it in regression. Finish this sentence: 'I'd like to find the cause of ...'"

Dorothy: "I would like to find the cause of my overwhelming fear that ... well, it isn't overwhelming, but there always seems to be a lot of fear." (begins to sob) "What it actually is, is when I'm trying to be assertive, I just can't seem to do it without crying. If I really need to be assertive, I need to work on it and get myself all prepared, and then I can do it, but that is really it. I don't know what I'm afraid of ... I'm afraid of people. I'm afraid of their reactions. It has something to do with what they'll think of me, but also it is their reactions. They might yell at me. I can't stand people yelling at me."

Dick: "Does that fear relate to any particular incident that you can recall?"

Dorothy: "I don't know. My dad may have yelled at me, but I have no memories of being with him. The man in whose home I lived was very gruff, and spoke in a gruff way, but I also knew that he loved me. I knew he would never hurt me, but yet I was still afraid that he might."

Dick: "So the fear was already there before you began to live with your foster parents at the age of 2½?"

Dorothy: "Yes. But I can't recall anything before that time."

Dick: "All right, if you're ready, Dorothy, I'd like to regress you now. Please connect the index finger and thumb of both hands in the mudra position; relax, lie back and make yourself comfortable. When I touch you on the forehead, your post-programming will be totally effective. You will feel the energy transfer from me to you, and you will immediately drop down into the deepest possible altered state of consciousness." (complete induction and instructions given)

Dick: "On the count of one, you will be back in the past, experiencing the cause of your current problem. Five, four, three, two, one. You are now there. Allow the impressions to come in, then speak up and tell me what you perceive and what is happening."

Dorothy: "I see my dad. He's angry about something, something I did."

Dick: "How old are you? You have the ability to perceive yourself."

Dorothy: "I think I'm two. Daddy's mad at me!" (sobbing)

Dick: "What did you do to make daddy mad?" (loudly)

Dorothy: (crying) "I wet my pants."

Dick: "Look at daddy. What's he saying? He's mad. You can see his face now. What is he doing, what's he saying?" (louder)

Dorothy: "'Damn kid!' that's what he's saying!" (crying) "I'm down low, on the floor. It's dark. Daddy's spanking me for wetting my pants."

Dick: "All right, Dorothy. You are only two years old, but you think very clearly. What are you thinking about right now?"

Dorothy: "He's mean! He hurt me really bad!" (crying and speaking loudly) **"I hate him! I hate him! I feel so alone and scared!"**

Dick: "All right, Dorothy, daddy has left now. He's gone. What is happening now?"

Dorothy: "It's dark in the room. I don't know where my mother is. I don't know ... I don't know!"

Dick: "Let go of this and talk to me about your mother, Dorothy."

Dorothy: "She doesn't love me. I'm too much trouble,

she can't take care of me."

Dick: "Too much trouble! What else?"

Dorothy: "She gets mad at me because I don't want to walk. I want her to carry me but she doesn't want to carry me." (sobbing)

Dick: "You like her to hold you, to show that she loves you?"

Dorothy: "Yes, but she says I'm too big for her to carry."

Dick: "All right, now listen closely to my words, Dorothy. After this, time passes. Then a time comes when you decide how you are going to relate to life. As a young child, you made some decisions about what the world is all about and how you are going to relate to the world. I want you to move to that time and tell me about it."

Dorothy: "I have to be a good little girl ... and be quiet. I have to do what other people tell me to do. I have to be nice. And not talk back. Be clean. Look nice." (pause)

Dick: "And if you do all of these things, Dorothy, what will happen?"

Dorothy: "People will like me!"

Dick: "And if they like you, maybe they will give you what mommy and daddy didn't give you, is that right?"

Dorothy: "Yes!" (sobbing)

Dick: "All right, now again, listen very closely to my words. As difficult as it is to imagine, I contend that you chose this situation. You chose to be born to unloving and uncaring parents, if that is reality. You purposely chose to put yourself in this environment as a balance, as a way to resolve karma. I contend that somewhere in your background, in another lifetime, is the cause. You must understand this in order to let go of the effect in your life. So I now want you to go back, way back, into a past life, back to a lifetime in which you did something that you would decide to balance in your present life." (Instructions are given to go back to the cause in another incarnation.)

Dick: "You are now there and vivid impressions are beginning to come in. What is happening?"

Dorothy: "There is a woman. A young woman ... and it's me. I'm leaving a baby outside a church. There is a big gate and a lot of stone. She's there with the baby." (crying) "She lays the baby down. It's all wrapped up in something. She's putting it on a stone porch in the doorway. And she just puts it down on the hard rock then turns and goes away." (gasping and crying)

Dick: "Let's follow her—where is she going?"

Dorothy: "She's going to a house. And, and ..." (sobbing) "She goes in, and there is a man in there. He is really mean. He's saying, 'Where were you? What did you do with that kid?'"

Dick: "What is she saying to him?"

Dorothy: "She says, 'You're never going to get her. I won't let you.' And he hits her!"

Dick: "I know this is painful, but I want you to totally experience it so you can let go of it. What else is happening?"

Dorothy: "I don't know what happened to her. She's gone. She's peaceful. She's gone. I don't know. I only know she gave up. She's gone ... gone."

Dick: "Okay, let go of this now and come back to the present." (instructions given) "Now, Dorothy, I want you to move up into your Higher-Self level of mind. From this level of awareness, you can tap into that vast part of your mind that you don't normally use. All of your past lives will be there, at your mental fingertips. And you will be able to look at your life from a transcendent viewpoint." (instructions given)

Dick: "You are now there, and I want you to obtain a full understanding of the karma involved in this situation. You are not a victim, Dorothy. You abandoned a child in that lifetime. Out of guilt programming, you chose to experience a similar situation in your current life as a balance. Everything has happened because you decided on a soul level that you needed to experience this in order to learn from it. You're teaching yourself. And I think you can let go of the effects now, if you are ready to forgive yourself. And you need to forgive your mother and father, because they were only playing the roles you chose for them to play. They were two souls with karmic configurations matching your own. Please meditate upon this for a while. I'm going to be quiet now."

Dorothy: "I forgive myself and I forgive my parents!" (sobbing)

Dick: "What was that, Dorothy? I didn't hear you."

Dorothy: "I FORGIVE MYSELF AND I FORGIVE MY PARENTS!" (very loud)

Inner-harmony automatically creates outer-harmony.

7.

Karmic Paths, Dharmic Directions And Soul Goals

An article in MASTER OF LIFE magazine.

The following information is **Master of Life** awareness which I attained through automatic writing in the fall of 1984. It was incorporated into the **Know Thy Higher Self** seminar which was offered in all our major market cities in 1985 and the spring of 1986. It was also released for individual personal exploration as part of a two-tape album titled **Why Are You Here?**

One of my initial reactions to these concepts was, "This is just one more teaching system among too many already existing teaching systems. People don·t need this kind of understanding, which certainly isn't any better than numerous systems being offered by numerous spiritual organizations."

As usual in meditations and automatic writing, I got my hands slapped. Based upon my notes made immediately following the sessions, this was the response: "Richard, you tend to want to kick people's crutches out from under them before they are ready to walk on their own. Your aversion to dogma and organizations does not always serve you. It is this kind of understanding that will encourage people to look beyond the systems. **Master of Life** concepts, as you have chosen to call them, are your path because they relate to your personality, and are the direct result of your lineage of lifetimes. The information about karmic paths, dharmic directions and soul goals is definitely Master of Life Awareness. There are many teachers and many paths because each spiritual communicator has a different lineage of preparation for the fulfillment of his dharma. One path is not purer or truer than another. They all lead to the same place. One path uses a little more technique, another a little more self-responsiblity, another a little more ritual, but that is only because different people respond to different paths. But all paths eventually lead to liberation. Some people will understand and relate better to your communications because of their past programming ... their lineage of lifetimes. And many who identify with your words have shared incarnations with you, or they share similar concerns on a soul level."

Having qualified my feelings about a teaching system, I must admit that when the three areas of exploration are synthesized, they very effectively point to your mission on the earth. I would, however, suggest that you do more than make conscious decisions based upon what you are about to read. Instead, meditate upon the ideas or use the tapes I've created, and ask a lot of your own questions.

There is a metaphysical axiom that says, "Man always follows the highest path of which he is really certain." Most likely, you are following the highest path of which you are really certain ... and the result is your current life, just the way it is. If your life isn't the way you would like it to be, suspend your beliefs for the next few minutes

63

and explore with an open, detached mind:

The Seven Karmic Paths

Let's carry our exploration of karma a little farther. Basically, there are seven karmic paths to follow. You can consciously decide which path you prefer ... or simply continue to live your life as you have up until now.

Which of the seven paths are you currently following? One path is not better than another path, it is just that some are longer and more painful. They will all eventually lead to the same place. The paths are not presented in order of desirability, although at first it may appear that way. When we get to the fifth and sixth paths, it could easily be open to argument as to which is the most karmically advantageous.

The first path is really **No Path.** It might be best expressed in poet William Blake's words when he said, "The road to excess leads to the palace of wisdom." Those on this path eventually, through experience and pain, will perceive what has value and what doesn't. Those on this path judge everything from a perspective of self, and often they have difficulty judging what action will result in harmony as opposed to disharmony. The No Path people appear to have little sense of balance and are usually unwilling to accept responsibility for their own lives.

The second path is called the **Beginning Path.** Beginning Path people are more responsible, but they enjoy having things "handed" to them. They want everything done "their way" and are materialistic and pleasure oriented. Chances are, those on the Beginning Path will be unlikely to have much interest in anything they can't eat, touch or enjoy.

The third path is the **Intermediate Path** and those who walk it are beginning to realize that there is an alternate reality. They might become interested in spiritual matters, but tend to be drawn to dogmatic thinking. While they are less "self" oriented, they usually remain very materialistic and pleasure centered.

The fourth path is the **Balanced Path** and those following it have an awareness of karma and carefully consider their actions because they are aware of the ramifications. They are beginning to comprehend unconditional love and are beginning to detach from the standard illusions about reality. They recognize that reality exists only in the way that you choose to experience it. It can be experienced as a hostile separateness or a tranquil oneness. Those on the Balanced Path don't repress their natural urges but refrain from excess.

The fifth path is the **Harmonious Path** and those who walk it require their outer life to be in harmony with their inner beliefs. They literally "live" their spiritual and self-actualized philosophy. They are beginning to incorporate unconditional love into their lives and have risen above blame and judgment. They accept "what is" and are well on the road to developing "detached mind." Vegetarianism is the most common dietary practice and most of those on the Harmonious Path practice meditation in some form.

The sixth path is the **Force of Will Path** and incorporates extreme discipline. It is the path of those in Zen monasteries, Yoga devotees and some priests . . . plus many others who center their lives around their spiritual faith. For many, this means extreme dietary practices and celibacy. The argument for following this path is that it is a rapid way to advance spiritually. The primary argument against this path is that it is undesirable to "drop out" of the "real" world and to repress your natural urges and desires, for in doing so, they will increase in intensity. Even if you manifest the self-discipline to deal with them in this life, you may generate a "karmic charge" that will

65

have to be dealt with in a future life.

The seventh path is the **Transcendental Path** and those who are on it are beyond seeking ... they are truly "in the world, but not of it." Only those who are highly evolved are capable of walking this path. They are living examples of "detached mind" and are dedicated to assisting others to find their way out of the darkness and into the spiritual light.

Dharma

Dharma is generally defined as "man's duty to oneself and to society." That means following a course of action that is right for you. By following your dharmic nature, or self-nature, you will most easily raise your vibrational level of awareness. When you follow your natural dharmic direction, you are responding to your own inner nature and, at the same time, this will usually be to the inner direction of a "greater whole."

Your karma conditions you through all your experiences to create the character required to carry out your dharma.

Let's look at the case of a political leader. Over many lifetimes, he developed his leadership abilities. In this life, the family and environmental circumstance into which he was born and educated are karmic. But his dharma is **governmental leadership**, and in addition to responding to his own inner nature, he responds to the voice of his country and the inner direction of a greater whole in accepting the leadership role.

We always have free will, so this leader may choose not to fulfill his dharma. He could refuse to listen to his inner direction ... or doubt the validity of what he perceives.

Usually, the best way to resolve your karma is to follow your dharmic direction ... the direction which is natural and destined for you.

The Seven Dharmic Directions

There are seven general dharmic directions. It is your purpose to explore one of these dharmic paths with a particular soul goal that you chose prior to your birth. The dharmic directions are:

1. Workforce involves the largest number of souls. This path encompasses the majority of general occupations as well as homemakers.

2. Military includes soldiers, all forms of police and militia, and those who enforce the laws of the country, state and city.

3. Service takes into consideration most religious workers, those in medical, welfare and social services, many practicing metaphysicians and those offering holistic health services.

4. Creativity includes artists, writers, poets, musicians, actors, and entertainers.

5. Science encompasses medical researchers, scientists, space technologists, and physicists.

6. Philosophy involves all who present theories about why man does what he does and how he might end suffering. Some church leaders would be included, along with philosophers and some metaphysical communicators.

7. Government includes political leaders, from the President of the United States to senators, governors, mayors, and anyone elected to office. It would also include those who take office by force through revolution.

Soul Goals

In addition to having chosen one of seven karmic paths and seven dharmic directions prior to your birth, I contend that you also chose one of the seven basic soul goals.

You may have more than one goal, but one will be most important; the next, secondary in importance, and so on.

Whether you consciously realize it or not, karmically, you have definite life goal priorities. These goals all amount to karmic self-testing, with an overall goal of spiritual growth.

The first soul goal is **Attain Knowledge.** This means attaining a particular area of knowledge which, when realized on a soul level, becomes wisdom. As an example, the desire for awareness could include one or more areas, such as direct knowledge of humility, devotion, sacrifice, selflessness, or perseverance.

The second soul goal is to **Open Spiritually** by the integration of spiritual awareness into the chosen dharmic direction. The form of the spirituality would depend upon the karmic path the individual has chosen to walk.

To Achieve Inner Harmony is the third soul goal and it means to be involved with the world and the accomplishment of the chosen dharmic duty while at the same time attaining balance and peace of mind.

Both elements of the fourth soul goal, **Attain Fame or Power,** are karmic rewards and offer unique opportunities to communicate awareness and exert leadership.

The fifth soul goal, **Learn Acceptance,** can be summarized as an awareness of "what is, is," for it is our resistance to what is that causes our suffering.

Provide Support is the sixth soul goal. This could range from the encouragement and support of another individual in the accomplishment of a jointly shared dharmic direction, to the support of an ideal or a philosophical or religious belief.

The seventh soul goal is **Develop Talent.** Talents are developed over many lifetimes, so the goal could be in the beginning, intermediary or advanced stage of a creative pursuit.

Synthesizing The Awareness

Let's carry our exploration of karma a little farther. Basically, there are seven karmic paths to follow. You can consciously decide which path you prefer ... or simply continue to live your life as you have up until now.

Remember, in regard to the karmic path you are currently walking, you have the free will to expand your awareness and consciously choose to walk a different path if you decide to do so. Also, your dharmic directions and soul goals are your karmic destiny. And you have the free will to fulfill your destiny or to avoid it.

For the first example, let's go back to the initial dharmic case I described earlier ... the man destined to fulfill his dharma in government. He was born with a dharmic direction of **government** with a goal of **fame or power,** a soul goal category which also includes leadership positions. This man has purposely chosen to walk the fourth or **balanced** karmic path as a result of a strong Christian upbringing and because, to fulfill his long-term political ambitions, he needs an "electable" background.

Let's explore the case of a famous singer who has been addicted to drugs for years. He earned the right in past lives to come into this life with a soul goal of **fame and power** and with a dharmic direction of **creativity.** In his earlier years, he was following the **intermediary** karmic path, but because of his drug addiction, is now on the **beginning** karmic path. This singer was given the opportunity to inspire and assist others in numerous ways but chose instead to bury himself in self-indulgence. His wife is an entirely different story. She is also a singer, but not as famous as her husband. She came into this life with a soul goal to **provide support,** with a secondary goal of **fame and power.** Her dharmic direction is also **creativity** and she is currently following a **balanced** karmic path. This woman stood by her husband through his years of addiction and has finally assisted him to overcome the dependency.

Another case history: Mary is married, has two children that are nearly grown, and sells real estate as a profession. Metaphysics is her primary interest in life and she is actively involved in a metaphysical organization. Her life revolves around her spiritual interests and she is on the **harmonious** karmic path. She was born with **workforce** dharmic direction and a soul goal of **attaining knowledge** in the area of **devotion.** From outward appearances, Mary is fulfilling her destiny and enjoying her life.

In another case, Jason is a 32-year-old freelance screenwriter who lives alone in Venice, California. Although quite talented, he makes very little money and experiences excessive frustration due to his unwillingness to accept the realities of his profession.

Jason is exploring an **intermediary** karmic path and he came into this life with **creativity** as his dharmic direction and a soul goal to **learn acceptance.** Although he doesn't realize it consciously, he is teaching himself to accept "what is" and all that it means.

Maria is a welfare worker in her early forties and has been divorced three times. Her divorces and the inequality and injustice she experiences in her daily work have caused Maria to look for deeper meaning in life. As a result, she walks a **balanced** karmic path and is aware that she came into this life with a dharmic direction of **service.** Her primary soul goal is to **achieve inner harmony.** From a higher perspective, she desires to learn to accept all the joy and love that life has to offer while at the same time learning to allow the negativity to flow through her without affecting her.

I'm sure you're getting the picture as to how the seven karmic paths, the seven dharmic directions and the seven soul goals all interrelate as a blueprint of your general life destiny.

Hopefully, this awareness will cause you to do some personal exploring and processing in regard to your life. Why are you here?

Bodhisattva

*The silence is broken
by the s-s-swish
of a Samurai sword*

severing illusion

*and it rolls across
the floor leaving
a bloody trail of*

truth.

*From the poetry book
RATTLESNAKE KARMA—1985*

71

8.

Master Of Life Dialogues

*About sexual masks, robot buttons, the three extreme emotions,
and not believing in God. Excerpts from
"The Master of Life Manual."*

Note: The following encounters are transcribed from
tape recordings between Dick and the participants at
Bushido® and **Master of Life®** Seminar Trainings. The
book includes a major section on metaphysical and
brain/mind awareness as well as 48 dialogues.

1.

Dick: "We have about 200 people in this training room
and three-fourths of you are women. How many of you
do not have a primary relationship in your life at this
time?" (almost half the hands are raised) "How many of
you really want to live alone?" (four hands are raised) "I
don't believe the four of you. I've worked with thousands
of people and have yet to find anyone who doesn't desire a
warm, joyful, fulfilling relationship in which they can
share experiences of mutual personal growth."

Trainee: "That's ridiculous. I've been married twice and
I don't see any value in it. I enjoy sex and now I can sleep

with any man I want to."

Dick: "When you said 'sex' just now, Linda, your body language became very anxious. What's going on with you and sex?"

Trainee: "Nothing. I love sex."

Dick: "Linda, you can play that game if you want to and hold onto your secret, or you can be open and honest and maybe find some answers of your own that will make your life work better."

Trainee: (Voice choking as tears form in her eyes) "The only problem is that I pretend I'm having an orgasm when I'm not. I want the man to think he's a really great lover so he'll ... uh ..."

Dick: "So he'll like you better."

Trainee: "Yeah. Is that so bad?"

Dick: "It's not bad or good. It's only that it keeps you from experiencing sex."

Trainee: "Oh, really!"

Dick: "Yes, **really!** You've been far too busy wearing a mask and pretending to be something you aren't. To experience something is to be totally focused on what is transpiring. It's impossible to have an orgasm while worrying about what he thinks."

Trainee: (crying) "I can get off fine afterwards, or the next day on my own."

Dick: "Of course. When you masturbate, you totally experience it. There are no fears or expectations blocking the experience. What I'm getting is that you aren't relating completely to anyone and that you're aching inside to do so."

Trainee: (crying) "Well, it just never works out. Every time I get close to a man, it falls apart. It's just too much trouble."

Dick: "What's the payoff in keeping things the way they are, Linda? For some fear-based reason, you are creating this situation exactly the way it is."

Trainee: (angrily) "I don't know!"

Dick: "Oh, yes, you do. You have all your own answers. **Why do you want to be alone, Linda? Why do you want to be alone?"**

Trainee: (crying and sobbing) "So I won't have to pretend all the time!"

Dick: "All right now, let go of this." (putting his arms around her and holding her) "Do you understand that the reason you've avoided getting involved in a primary relationship isn't valid?"

Trainee: "Yes, I do see that. In fact, I really want a relationship, just not a painful one."

Dick: "Now, when I'm talking with Linda, I'm talking to every single person in this training room. Linda has been wearing a mask, pretending to be something she isn't. When we do that, it takes a great deal of energy, thus we're only able to wear the mask for limited periods of time. For Linda, wearing this mask is so draining that it's easier to be by herself than to be in a relationship. Because of this, she subconsciously destroys every potential relationship. Once Linda decides that it's okay to be direct and honest in her communications with the men in her life, she'll probably allow herself to be open to involvement in a relationship."

Trainee: "But I feel that I need to make the men feel good about themselves."

Dick: "I believe the greatest gift you can give to another human being is to be all of who you are. If you are yourself and totally experience your sexual involvements, you'll probably start enjoying sex again and the men will automatically feel good about your enjoyment. But let's just say for a moment that you pretend successfully and the man falls in love with you. Does he love you or the mask you're wearing, Linda?"

Trainee: "The mask, I guess."

Dick: "Of course. And one day the mask would become too heavy. You'd take it off and he'd scream about the fact that you'd changed; you weren't the girl he married."

Trainee: "Ohhh. That's exactly what happened in both my marriages."

Dick: "Linda, be yourself. Be just what you are and nothing else. That way, if love develops, it's based on the way you really are. If it doesn't, there aren't any illusions to be painfully dissolved later."

2.

Dick: "We've talked a great deal about how the mind works like a computer, and since we are mind, that makes us machines ... robots. We all have computer buttons; when they get pushed, you become a robot and demonstrate your automatic responses. You see, a robot has no choice in the way it acts. It has wiring and circuits constructed so that, when a button is pushed, it reacts according to its programming. And in so many areas of your life you're a robot; that's a major reason your life doesn't work as well as it could.

"You can't change what you don't recognize, so it is time to recognize your automatic responses and learn to override them. It's time to stop going on 'tilt' when someone or something pushes one of your buttons. 'Tilt' is when you stop functioning rationally.

"All right. Go up to your center." (altered-state induction given) "Let's explore a few of your buttons. What causes you to react? As I ask you some questions, be straight with yourself and trust the very first thought that comes into your mind. What causes you to become angry quickly?" (pause) "What embarrasses you?" (pause) "What really irritates you about your mate?" (pause) "What really bothers you in your career?" (pause) "What

75

causes you to become fearful?" (pause) "What pushes your sexual buttons off and on?" (pause) "Does what other people think control you in any particular area?" (pause) "What is it that you fear them thinking or knowing?" (pause) "How does what other people think manipulate you?" (pause)

"Can you get that you've been programmed? Brainwashed from birth to worry about what other people think? You grew up worrying about what others think. Your parents worried about what other people thought. But what others think may not be in your best interest. What **YOU** think is most important. There is really no such thing as right and wrong, ethical and unethical, moral and immoral. A society, which is a group of people, agrees upon what terminology to use regarding a particular action; maybe they agree to call it moral or immoral. That doesn't make it either moral or immoral, it only makes it what that group labels moral or immoral. Their naming it one thing or another cannot change what it is. In some countries, eating cattle is immoral. In other countries, the word 'rape' is not a part of the language—not even a concept, for the men assume the right to take women by force whenever they desire to do so. In some areas of the world, open sexuality is considered moral and beautiful.

"When living in a society, we must be willing to accept the consequences of our actions regarding the laws of the society, yet most of the conflicts with the opinions of others are not legal issues. It may be ill-advised for you to allow the opinions of others to push your reaction buttons and cause you to repress what you really are. Think about how this relates to your life." (pause)

"Okay, we've explored just a few of your buttons. When they get pushed, you react quickly, and this will rarely be in your best interests. You know this. You are reacting to the button, to the old programming, not to what is. You need to become consciously aware of all your buttons, and when you awaken, we're going to explore a technique to hold back in your immediate inclination to react."

3.

Dick: "In regard to your buttons: I'm not saying to repress what you are, I am simply saying that if you hold back in your initial inclination to react immediately to anger, fear, or adoration, your life will work better. The idea is to catch yourself long enough to think about your reaction.

"A martial arts student is taught to keep his 'mind like calm water,' because if he allows himself to become angry or fearful, he greatly reduces his potential to win in an encounter. To keep your mind like calm water accurately reflects everything within striking range.

"Instead of reacting to extreme emotions, go into a calm inner space where you calculate the best response to get what you want. The goal is to win the game, not to be right. But as a robot, your subconscious computer has one primary goal: **survival.** It achieves that goal by comparing the present to the past. This means, in essence, that your subconscious computer says it is all right for you to live your life just as you do.

"It has survived so far and it knows that it did it by being right. According to computer logic, it **has** to be right. Of course, you know consciously that you aren't always right … but your subconscious doesn't. So, it responds to programming and you get to be right, but you lose the game. When you are challenged, you become indignant. Your button is pushed and you react quickly. And, as you probably know from experience, this is rarely in your best interest.

77

"You are reacting to the button, **not** to what is. So you need to be consciously aware of your programming instead of subconsciously reacting to it. It is part of the **Bushido** code that 'the strong are patient.' Patience in this case means to hold back in your immediate inclination to respond to the extreme emotions of anger, fear, and adoration."

Trainee: "I don't understand why you include adoration as one of the three extreme emotions."

Dick: "Okay, let's say you are married, Louise, but you meet someone and your infatuation is so intense that you respond to the offer to go to bed with him. You've broken an agreement, so at the very least, you're going to have sacrificed self-esteem, which is negative programming. Or maybe your husband finds out about it and the result is a weakened marriage. Or, in today's society, the result could be AIDS or some other sexual disease."

Trainee: "But how can you overcome a lifetime of conditioning to obtain the kind of control you're talking about?"

Dick: "It would have to begin with the desire, wouldn't it? You would have to realize that you'll be better served by changing the way you react to others. Next, a technique such as 'mudra' can be of great supportive value.

"Touch your index finger and thumb together to form the mudra position. This is a post-programming technique which can be fully conditioned in about three weeks if you include it every day as part of your self-hypnosis or meditation session. In an altered state, tell yourself, 'whenever I purposely connect my index finger and thumb, I will immediately become calm and peaceful. The mudra finger position is a conditioned response key to my subconscious mind and when I use it, I will immediately experience an internal balance and harmony that will allow me to override my extreme emotions, giving me time to think calmly about my reactions. And every time I give myself this suggestion, every time I use the mudra finger positioning, it will become more powerful.'"

4.

Trainee: "It took a while, but now I can really understand what you mean when you say, 'Don't believe in God, experience God.' But I was raised Catholic and I'm still stuck on heaven and hell."

Dick: "To me, heaven and hell are symbols that relate to the here and now. When you experience peace, balance and harmony, you experience heaven. When you are disharmonious and fearful, you experience hell. Heaven and hell are reflections of your consciousness."

Trainee: "I like that. I realize it isn't part of this seminar, but what do you think about the forthcoming antichrist?"

Dick: "It is my truth that the antichrist is already here and has been for a very long time. An antichrist is one who exploits in the name of Christ. Who would that be?"

Trainee: "The pope, priests and preachers!"

Dick: (smiles)

You are the living
result of
your beliefs.

9.

Controversial Questions

From a continuing column in MASTER OF LIFE magazine.

Q.

John McKenna of Houston, Texas, writes to say that he has devoted the last three months to metaphysical studies. "It has literally changed my outlook on life," he explains, but he goes on to question a basic premise: "I keep reading that the world is **maya** [*illusion*], and I just can't buy that. What is your opinion?"

A.

It is the Buddhists who primarily talk of "maya," but you are taking them literally and thus misinterpreting their meaning of the word. They do not mean that trees or mountains or cities are unreal. They mean the world exists as you interpret it. You see it through your eyes and relate to it based upon your past programming. It is your thoughts about the world that create the negative and the positive but both are illusions. They are not "what is," because your neighbor sees and experiences a different world, and your parents another, and your lover yet another.

The Buddhists often talk of people as magicians because it is your dreams that create your world. "Thoughts are things and they create" is a metaphysical axiom founded in fact. It's why self-programming tapes are so effective. When you change your programming, you change your world.

Some metaphysicians accept that the real world is God, but that we are blocked from experiencing God because we create and project our own viewpoints to the degree that we live in illusion.

Q.

"You've ruined my week," begins a letter from Susan Soble of Queens, New York. "In fact, you've probably ruined more than one week. I just finished reading your new book, **Enlightenment Transcripts.** In it, you say 'that which you resist, you become.' I can't get that thought out of my mind because there are a lot of people I **really** resist. I resist punkers with purple Mohawk haircuts, I resist homosexuals, and I hate foreign cab drivers who can't understand enough English to get me where I am paying them to take me. Obviously, I am not going to become punk, gay and foreign in the time I have left in this life, but now you've got me worried about my next life. I'm deciding right now, I'm not coming back."

A.

You absolutely won't have to come back, Susan ... unless, of course, on the other side you have more spiritual awareness and decide to return! Think about the concept. I contend that we are here on the physical plane to fulfill our dharma, resolve our karma, and in the process, to raise our vibrational rate by acting positively, with love and compassion, opposed to acting negatively with anger and fear. All negativity is actually fear, so you can simplify your purpose in life to the idea of letting go of fear and expressing unconditional love.

Resistance is **always** based in fear. So your resistance to punks, gays and foreigners is obviously an area of fear you need to learn about and deal with. Maybe it can be condensed to your unwillingness to accept those who are different. That which you resist, you become ... unless you learn what it is you need to learn. Ideally, we learn through love and wisdom, but if we don't have enough love and wisdom, we can always learn by directly experiencing the consequences of our attitudes and actions. Can you imagine living in A.D. 2222 as a gay freak who migrates to another country and has trouble learning the language?

Q.

L.N. Weinstein of New York City writes: "In your condensed book on tape, **Breaking The Chains of Illusion,** the questions you ask about masks as 'patterned behavior' have changed my life. But I am having a problem with the section about repression. You say that when a person represses sexually, he becomes angry. I just can't buy that. I see celibacy as spiritual advancement."

A.

History will easily support the idea that the more you repress sex, the more angry and violent you tend to become. Sexual energy can thus be used very effectively by those who direct armies. If the soldiers have no opportunity to experience sex, their energy and anger can be channeled into the battle.

Celibacy is demanded by most cults, and encouraged by many religions, so you think it is spiritual. These organizations know that sex is such a powerful force, it can't be successfully repressed. Thus, when the followers fail to successfully repress their sexuality, they feel guilty. It is much easier to control guilty peole. And when they continue to fail, they lose self-esteem. It is even easier to control people who have low self-esteem. The followers accept that they are sinners and the guru or church becomes their only hope of redemption. It's a very successful ploy.

I say you are here on earth to raise your level of awareness by interacting harmoniously with physical reality. When you reject an aspect of physical reality and pretend it doesn't exist, you are not living a life of "total involvement." Until you can go through an entire lifetime with total involvement and no fear responses, you will continue to reincarnate.

From a karmic overview, there is also the idea that you become what you resist—if not in this life, in the next. So, if you resist sexuality in this life, you'll just have to come back and deal with it in the next. By then, the repression may have become perverted.

Q.

A seminar participant said to me, "There is simply no way that child molestation could be karmic. I can't accept that. How could you karmically justify this hideous crime perpetrated upon an innocent child?"

A.

Either karma is the basis of reality or it isn't. There is no halfway karma. I accept that karma is what is. And if that's accurate, then **everything** is karmic.

As Gibran said in **The Prophet,** "The murdered is as guilty as the murderer." He was speaking from a karmic perspective, and saying that the man who was murdered had murdered someone else in a past life. By experiencing the direct consequences of his actions, he learns to value life and resolves his karma in the process. Hopefully, he intuitively learns on a soul level, and will never forget this painful lesson.

As hard as it may be to accept, a child too has a long

history of past lifetimes, and has reincarnated to resolve his karma and fulfill his dharma. If, in a past life, he has mistreated, abandoned or molested children, karma must be balanced.

I recall hearing in a seminar, the past-life case history of a man in his mid-thirties who had been molested as a young boy by a gay uncle. While seeking the cause through hypnotic regression, he reexperienced a lifetime in medieval Europe as a member of a savage, wandering band. While raiding villages, they often stole young men from their families, to be used as slaves and for sexual pleasure when women were not available. In understanding the cause, this man was finally able to forgive his uncle.

Of course, his uncle will have karma to balance at some time in this life or in a future life. There are always others with karmic configurations matching our needs for learning experiences, and we will unconsciously seek them out to learn our lessons.

Q.

An often-asked question, both in seminars and in letters, is, "Why do you use the spiritual white light protection technique at the beginning of all your tapes and before every seminar session? Is there something to be afraid of?"

A.

First, I use it because it is a beautiful and extremely powerful invocation which doubles as a "visualization exercise" to prepare you for the subjective experience. Second, I use it to assure that there will be no influence from earthbound entities.

You cannot be influenced by an entity with a vibrational rate lower than your own. So most metaphysical people certainly don't "need" this protection. But if your aura has been weakened by drug-taking, excessive alcohol, illness, or depression, your vibrational rate can be temporarily reduced. My "god-light" technique offers protection from any undesirable unseen influences.

Even being extremely negative or hateful can lower your vibrational rate, until you regain your internal balance. If your natural protection is down, I bring it back up while I am working with you to assure only accurate perceptions and positive programming.

I always suggest that those who take drugs, drink to excess, experience illness or are in an extremely negative frame of mind, use the technique several times a day while they are wide awake and going through their daily activities. An earthbound entity can influence you as easily while you are fully conscious as when you are in an altered state.

Q.

On some recent TV and radio interview shows, I've been asked a great deal about the Sedona psychic energy vortexes. Our seminars there have attracted worldwide attention, and since the release of the Sedona book and video, the subject has become one of the hot metaphysical issues. The skeptical question is usually phrased something like this: "Oh, come on, Richard, you can't measure this energy with any known technical instrument. It sounds to me like a snake oil scam to attract true believers."

A.

Even the medical nursing profession has finally accepted the validity of the technique of the laying on of hands to heal. It does work, yet there is no way to technically measure the healing energy. Kirlian photography shows this energy in abundance before the healing and dissipated after the session. We are talking about a subtle, psychic energy that doesn't fit into existing categories at this time.

Sometimes the interviewer will ask, "If I went there, can you guarantee me that I'd experience this energy?"

And I respond by asking, "Are you interested in psychic development? Have you ever attempted to receive psychic, subjective impressions?"

"No," they invariably answer.

"I have a friend who plays in a major symphony orchestra," I continue. "Do you think you have the subtle musical understanding that he has?"

"No, probably not."

"And I doubt that you would have the ability to perceive the subtle psychic energy in the Sedona vortexes on the level of a metaphysically oriented individual."

And I always end this aspect of any interview by saying, "In a couple of hours, I could teach you how to psychically perceive in the vortexes, if you're open enough to explore. I don't want anyone to take my word on the existence of the energy. Go see for yourself."

Q.

A letter from Alan MacKenzie, Baltimore, Maryland, asks: "You and many other spiritual teachers continually say, 'We are all **one**!' Obviously, we are all individuals, not one."

A.

There are many ways to view the concept of oneness, but I'll share my favorite: Within the 90 percent of our mind that we do not normally use is our Higher Self. And within Higher Self is the "collective unconscious"—the collective awareness of all mankind, all souls, living and discarnate. Thus we are all connected and the living result of this awareness. We are all one.

This is the God level, the level of supreme enlightenment ... of liberation. And although most of us are not yet able to maintain extended contact with this level of our totality, we can be influenced if we are open. It also explains why, throughout history, writers, philosophers and inventors have come up with the same concepts or discoveries at the same time. In these cases of simultaneous discovery, mankind as a group energy has experienced the prerequisite awareness necessary for the birth of the new idea. So the idea is there, just waiting for discovery by those most attuned to the particular vibration.

Q.

One of the most frequently asked questions at seminars is, "Exactly what is the Higher Self?"

A.

First, as I've written for years and often proven in groups, when you successfully access Higher Self, you have all knowledge at your mental fingertips. You have awareness of your past lives and the present as it relates to you or anyone else you care to psychically know. How could this be? Because you are accessing the totality—the entire energy gestalt named "God." In other words, your Higher Self is the collective awareness of the gestalt. It is The All That Is ... The Oneness.

So, is your Higher Self the same as my Higher Self? Of course. We are both part of the same energy gestalt, part of God. People argue that their Higher Self is a separate entity. This could be accurate if viewed as a superior intelligence/awareness but that is so limiting. Your Higher Self isn't your spirit guide or a Master teacher; it is the awareness of all that has ever been, all that is, and all that can potentially be.

10.

Belief In The End Times

An article in WHAT IS newspaper.

When people ask me if I really believe in reincarnation, I respond by saying, "NO! I accept reincarnation as my philosophical basis of reality as a result of my **experience.** After 19 years of verifying past-life regressions and valid pieces of supportive psychic information, I have no doubts that past lives are influencing my present life. A belief is your opinion. Experience is your reality!"

A belief is something you don't know. You may think you know. You might even be willing to stake your life on the fact that you know. But you don't know. You believe your husband is faithful; you believe there is a God; you believe in reincarnation ... but there is no way to know for sure if your belief is based upon what is. Belief is a prejudice without any experience to support it.

Religions retain their followers by convincing them to believe in hell ... the end of the world ... and that those not of their denomination are a threat. This is well expressed by Indian spokesman Vine Deloria, Jr., in his book, **God Is Red:** "Without the ability to invoke emotion, to create fear and anxiety, to promise instantaneous relief from such fears, they are helpless. It is by artificially creating that solitary individual through deliberate manipulation of his emotions that they give credence to their vision of the Christian religion. They are notably absent in the solutions of social problems, in the ongoing work of local communities, and in the examination of the nature of human personality and its problems."

Sadly enough, many metaphysical people have accepted the same fears. Actually, rather than merely accepting, they seem to eagerly embrace a forthcoming pole shift, war and the end of the world as we know it. There is no subject that creates as much interest when I speak in public. And when I tell my audience that the whole idea has been cooked up to sell religion and books, many of them get mad at me. There is a dark side to their personalities that wants this negative belief to manifest.

The reason is probably best described by Eric Hoffer in his book, **The True Believer:** "There is a deep reassurance for the frustrated in witnessing the downfall of the fortunate and the disgrace of the righteous. They see in a general downfall an approach to the brotherhood of all. Chaos, like the grave, is a haven of equality. Their burning conviction that there must be a new life and a new order is fueled by the realization that the old will have to be razed to the ground before the new can be built. Their clamor for a millenium is shot through with a hatred for all that exists, and a craving for the end of the world."

It is the frustrated and unfulfilled who accept the idea of the forthcoming end of the world. They may accept the belief because a psychic said so, or because they read it in a book. Yet I interviewed eight of the top psychics and metaphysical communicators in the country for a tape entitled, "The End Times & Armageddon," and these people didn't accept the ideas. Even Charles Thomas Cayce, Ph.D., who directs the Association for Research and Enlightenment, said he doesn't foresee any cataclysmic events or end time conflicts during our lifetime.

"Then why does a good psychic, or channel medium, say the end times are coming?" I am asked. I respond by relating several facts. First, most psychics are not very accurate. The highest accuracy rate I've ever seen is 85 percent and that certainly isn't projectable. Alan Vaughan, one of the top psychics in the land, once monitored all the psychic predictions in a January issue of the *National Enquirer.* Twelve months later, not one single prediction had proven to be accurate.

Another reason mediums receive this information is, since so many people believe in the forthcoming cataclysms, the thought forms are "in the air" and the mediums misinterpret them as prophecy. Future events simply are not predestined to this degree this far in advance. In her latest book, Ruth Montgomery has some explanations as to why some of her guides' past predictions didn't come to pass, and she modifies some of the others.

We can make predictions based upon the current conditions, but as those conditions change, the future potential changes. Based upon current trends and conditions, I might predict major monetary problems for our country. Inflation appears to be coming back. Over 1400 banks are on the Federal Deposit Insurance problem list, and over 100 banks have failed in 1986. Forty-three percent of the Savings and Loans in the U.S.A. are either insolvent or have less capital than the legal requirement. The Farm Credit System is near collapse; Wall Street firms are selling junk bonds; the repurchase market and consumer debt could all collapse. But if enough people act, this nightmare can be averted.

It is not a predestined event. We have the free will to decide our own fate. And our actions may affect not only this life, but our lives that follow.

"Well, I believe the predictions of Nostradamus are accurate!" I've had many people tell me.

"Oh, have you studied his writings and drawn definite conclusions?" I ask.

"No, but I saw the movie narrated by Orson Welles," they tell me. Or, "I've read a book, and the author has done the research."

And, as with the biblical Book of Revelations, everyone interprets the writings in their own way, in relation to their own time, and usually quite differently than the next person working with the very same material.

And people tend to believe what they want to believe, what they have already imagined. The frustrated hear in these predictions an echo of their own musings. The predestined events offer them a way to be rid of an unwanted self. Their own lives are so drab and undesirable that they look to an earth cleansing as a chance at a new life ... rebirth!

It is not unlike some of the recently exposed subliminal techniques used to attract more buyers for hard liquor. When symbols of death are subliminally airbrushed into the ice cubes in magazine ads, liquor buyers are more apt to respond positively to the ad. Their real desire is for self-destruction.

Belief doesn't work! And always, deep within the believer, is an undercurrent of doubt. People are good at covering it up, even to the point of forgetting it is there. But doubt always has the potential of surfacing if questioned. Thus believers are afraid to listen to anything contrary to their beliefs.

The churches know this, so they ban books and condemn ideas that might allow their followers to question what is. Buddha said, "Do not believe, for if you believe, you will never know. If you really want to know, don't believe." That doesn't mean to **dis**believe—disbelief is simply another belief. Both devout Christians and atheists are "believers."

Buddha also offers the solution, "Come and see!" It is an invitation to directly experience . . . and to go into yourself to see and feel experientially. It is an invitation to experiment.

To create a new world, we must first attain freedom and independence ourselves. We must "know" ourselves. This requires an incredibly alert mind, for what **is** is always changing. To follow the continually changing what is, you must not be attached to any absolute belief, or any standardized pattern of action.

Even to believe in God will not serve you. Seek to directly experience God, and to experience that you are also God, and you will experience transformation. A Master of Life knows that unhappiness and failure are self-inflicted, and happiness and success are self-bestowed. In other words, you create your own reality. I don't want you to believe that. I'd like to have you experience it.

11.

Bodhisattva

*The Six Perfections and the Ten Precepts of Moral Conduct.
An article in MASTER OF LIFE magazine.*

The symbol of the **Bushido® Training Seminar** is
Manjusri—the Bodhisattva of Wisdom riding a lion,
holding a sword of wisdom that cuts through delusion.
Bodhisattva is a Sanskrit term meaning "one who
supports others in achieving enlightenment."

According to Zen, these individuals have reached the
point of liberation and have decided not to step off the
wheel of reincarnation; instead, they have chosen to
continue incarnating to serve other living beings until all
are free.

The term is composed of *bodhi*, meaning "perfect
wisdom," and *sattva*, meaning "an intelligent being whose
actions make for harmony." As we spiritually evolve, our
progress can be divided into three phases. The first is
"attached" mind, which is rooted in self and clings to the
world. The attached mind is filled with the fear-based
emotions of selfishness, envy, egotism, jealousy, greed,
vanity, hate, possessiveness, malice, hostility, desire for

revenge, resentment, anxiety, need to control, and anger.

The second phase is when an individual begins to develop "detached mind" ... and this is the beginning of the Bodhisattva phase. During this period, he learns to let go of fear and to express unconditional love. At the completion of the phase, he will have fulfilled his dharma, resolved his karma and will not have to return to the earth plane except by choice, to be of service as a Bodhisattva.

The third phase of spiritual evolution is to become a Spiritual Master. A Master usually leaves the earth plane but continues to assist people from the other side. To be a Master is to attain the ultimate state of consciousness. It is said, if you serve as a Bodhisattva when your own work on earth is done, you will be "a window to God forever."

I contend that once someone becomes involved in metaphysical and New Age learning, they have crossed over into the Bodhisattva phase of their spiritual evolution. As a guideline for self-advancement, Masters long ago established **Six Perfections** for the seeker, and **Ten Precepts** of moral conduct to accelerate the process of liberation.

The Ten Precepts

1. Not to kill: This means not only not to literally kill, but to help yourself to really live by developing "detached mind."

2. Not to steal: This means not only not to literally steal, but to give to others. In Zen, if you don't practice donation (giving), you are stealing—from yourself and your own potential illumination.

3. Not to misuse sexuality: This means that the person having sex with another must consider his own happiness, that of his companion and of the third person who will be most affected by his act. If these three concerned people can be satisfied, then sex falls within the natural law of human beings.

4. Not to lie: This means not only not to lie to others, but to avoid the lie of pride.

5. Not to misuse intoxicants: This means not to be drunken or to harm the health of your body or mind by using intoxicants to excess.

6. Not to slander: This means to shun gossip, slander and verbal abuse of any kind. Be truthful and loving with your words.

7. Not to insult: This means never to purposefully hurt someone else with words. They will always come back to you through cause and effect.

8. Not to covet: This means not wanting to get more than you need; not being greedy and ungenerous toward others who may be in greater need than yourself.

9. Not to anger: Anger is always a protection against pain, but once you realize the pain exists only because you allow it to exist, you cease to become angry.

10. Not to slander the All That Is: This means to become aware that we are the All.

The Six Perfections

The Paramitas of the Bodhisattva date back to A.D. 499–569. Bodhisattva is sometimes explained as "someone who practices the six paramitas." The first five perfections are of the mind, including the heart and will. Those who have developed detached mind will have these five, and will have experienced liberation. They are then ready for the great adventure of "transcendental wisdom."

1. Giving: There are three kinds of giving: The giving of materials, the giving of awareness and the giving of "non-afraidness." The giving of materials usually means money, clothes, food, or labor. This giving is usually directed to churches, temples, causes, or organizations assisting the needy.

The giving of awareness means to share awareness

95

that will lead others down the path to liberation. The knowledge should never be forced upon another, but always take the time and effort to plant seeds in the minds of those who are receptive.

The giving of "non-afraidness" means to be willing to risk yourself to save others from disaster or misfortune.

2. Keep the precepts: This means to live by the ten precepts already related. To break the precepts results in karma which must be balanced before we can evolve further spiritually.

3. Perseverance: The world includes suffering: separation of loved ones, illness, old age, loneliness, accidents, guilt, monetary hardship, and unfulfilled desires. Yet we must persevere and rise above the sufferings, physically as well as mentally.

4. Assiduity: This means to exert the diligence not to do anything disharmonious and to do everything harmoniously. Nothing is completed without diligence. Because we are part of society, we must work for money, name, power, and position; but as a Bodhisattva, we realize that our real work has nothing to do with these things, and should be directed to creating harmony on this earth.

5. Meditation: By going within on a regular basis, you become attuned to that which is not manifest and awaken the True Self, which is the universe.

6. Transcendental wisdom: This is wisdom that transcends the knowledge of things and of the mind. It transcends all dualities to become illumination.

12.

Eva
False Guilt Regression

From the book "Past-Life Therapy In Action,"
co-authored with Lauren Leigh Taylor.

If my subject has a severe physical problem which is also associated with depression or emotional troubles, experience has taught me not to be satisfied with a "cause" that does not include **guilt.** In my years of working with past-life therapy, it has become obvious that guilt carries with it the harshest of punishments in a future life. It is also through the exploration of many cases of **false guilt** that I became convinced that there is no judgmental entity on high who doles out an "eye for an eye"! If God punishes, he certainly wouldn't punish without reason. Yet we obviously punish ourselves when we need to atone for a past misdeed . . . even if we are mistaken. Even if we didn't do anything wrong, although we think we did.

The following exploration took place in an "All You Are Capable of Being" seminar in Maui, Hawaii. The group numbered just 22, allowing ample time to get to know each other personally and to explore some exciting case histories in more detail than possible in most seminars.

Eva Johnson, 51, of Glen Arm, Maryland, has given me full permission to relate the details of her situation and to use the word-for-word transcription of the past-life regression. Eva's problem can be summarized as, **all her life being hungry, but never being in a position to eat.**

As one of three children in Germany, Eva had a strict father who was determined that his daughter read and write before other children. Whenever she could not comply with his wishes, he would punish her by withholding food. Although she was attempting to do work beyond her mental development, she was starved most of the time. Eva was five when World War II started, and 13 when it ended. In her words, she explains, "We were going through progressive starvation, until finally our food was cut off altogether. Survival became our reality and it never ended. It got worse rather than better. And even after the war, it didn't end. It continued on for two more years. I had to beg from American soldiers or steal in order to stay alive."

As an adult, Eva emigrated to the United States, where she started her own very successful business. But, once more, instead of being able to eat in an environment of plenty, she found that if she ate in excess of 1,000 calories a day, her weight ballooned. She explained, "If all you can eat is 1,000 calories, you are always hungry. So, what I've been doing is eat normally for 60 days and gain an immense amount of weight. Then I fast for 30 days and lose it again. Even this isn't working anymore. I think I'll have to eat for 30 days and fast for 30 days."

For the regression, Eva laid comfortably in a recliner with the rest of the seminar participants in a semicircle around her. I sat beside her, and after the hypnotic induction, instructed, "I want you to go back to the cause of your overweight and hunger problem. It may lie in your current life or in a past life, but together, we are now going to go back to the cause and allow forgotten awareness to flow down out of your subconscious and into your conscious mind...." (Instructions given.)

Dick: "Speak up and tell me what you perceive ... what's happening?

Eva: "I am afraid." (She begins to tremble.)

Dick: "What are you afraid of?"

Eva: "Of a trap, in the snow. All of us. We didn't get out before it snowed."

Dick: "Are you there with others? How many?"

Eva: "Oh, maybe 30 or 40 others."

Dick: "Okay, tell me everything you can about the situation."

Eva: "We were trying to get through before the snow came. We didn't make it. Now we're stuck. We can't get out."

Dick: "What was your mode of transportation?"

Eva: "Wagon and walking."

Dick: "How old are you?"

Eva: "I am 10."

Dick: "What's your name?"

Eva: "Mary."

Dick: "All right, Mary. You're 10 years of age, you're trapped with 30 or 40 others. Were you part of a wagon train? Is that it?"

Eva: "Yes."

Dick: "Okay, tell me about what's happening now. Tell me more about it."

Eva: "Well, we ... it's very cold, and we have nothing to eat."

Dick: "Okay, what was the name of your group?"

Eva: "Uh, Donner?"

Dick: "Yes. Okay, I want you to move forward to something very important on the count of three: one,

99

two, three."

Eva: "My grandfather died. He just died."

Dick: "Is your mother there? Your father, are they there?"

Eva: "My father is not here."

Dick: "Your father, where's your father?"

Eva: "I think he was waiting for us on the other side. . . . I don't know."

Dick: "All right, you were traveling with your mother and your grandfather, is this correct?"

Eva: "Yeah, and my sister, and my brothers, and Grandfather died."

Dick: "What is your mother telling you? Will you bury your grandfather?"

Eva: "Well, we don't say, we don't say that. They're feeding us now, they're feeding us now."

Dick: "They're feeding you."

Eva: "And they don't want us to know that it's Grandfather. I just know it is. I just know it is, and I shouldn't be eating this." (Eva is shaking and tears are rolling down her cheeks.)

Dick: "Are you hungry, Mary?"

Eva: "Yeah."

Dick: "Very, very hungry? I want you to experience the hunger. How does it feel to be that hungry?"

Eva: "It doesn't matter, nothing matters."

Dick: "Yes, it does matter. You're eating. You're hungry, and it hurts. Tell me about it. I want you to totally experience this. You're going to experience it and you're going to come out the other side." (Additional time taken to experience the hunger.) "Now tell me, what's it feel like to be this hungry?"

Eva: "It's awful! Your own sister and brother become your enemies, that's all it is, is hunger. Nothing else, there's nothing else."

Dick: "All right, we're going to move forward now. Mary, you're moving deeper into the winter. Tell me what is happening now."

Eva: "More of the older people are disappearing."

Dick: "They're disappearing, or they're dying? What's happening to the older people?"

Eva: "I don't think they're just dying any more. I think, I think the others are killing them."

Dick: "You think they're killing the old people to eat them?"

Eva: "I think ... I really think so, yes."

Dick: "All right. Time ... how is your time spent? What do you do with your day? I want to know everything that's happening."

Eva: "Inside of a hole, inside of a snow hole."

Dick: "A snow hole, okay."

Eva: "We just huddle together because it is very cold."

Dick: "So this is how you spend your entire day? Huddling together to keep warm?"

Eva: "Children, their mothers and others."

Dick: "How? Do you live individually, or are you in one encampment? How is it set up? How many of you are left now, and how is it set up?"

Eva: "Well, there are just two families left. But it's not all one family in the whole. It's mostly just children and the women left. And I think everybody knows now, everybody knows now, except the very little ones. I shouldn't be eating this."

Dick: "And you are eating. What do you feel about eating these people, Mary?"

Eva: "They all do, everybody knows. ..."

Dick: "What do you feel about it, Mary? What do you feel about eating the people?"

Eva: "I think it's awful."

Dick: "And you're doing it. What do you feel about

101

doing it when you think it's awful?" (I purposely push her to cause her to release repressed emotions.)

Eva: "Part of me thinks it's all right, and part of me thinks it's not. And mother says it's all right."

Dick: "Okay, I want you to move forward in time a little further, a little further, Mary. More time is passing, deeper and deeper into the winter. What's happening now?"

Eva: "There aren't too many left. Just the women and children. Two men."

Dick: "Two men?"

Eva: "And they're afraid of the women. They have a hole by themselves."

Dick: "The men have their own hole, because they're afraid of the women?"

Eva: "Yeah."

Dick: "Why are they afraid of the women?"

Eva: "I guess they want to keep their children alive."

Dick: "The women want to keep their children alive, what does that mean?"

Eva: "They will want the men ... to eat them." (She begins to cry and shudder.)

Dick: "Let go of this now, and without pain or emotion, on the count of three, I want you to move now to the very last day of your life in this past life we're now examining. You will not have died, you will not have crossed over into spirit. But it's now the last day of your life, and I want you to tell me what's happening."

Eva: "I am now a grandmother and I'm old."

Dick: "Well, Mary, I want you to look back on your life, and I want you to tell me about what happened. You were trapped, as part of the Donner party, in the snow. So you escaped, is this correct?"

Eva: "Yeah. Spring. Spring came."

Dick: "Spring came and you survived. How many

survived?"

Eva: "Not many, not too many. Fifteen? Twenty?"

Dick: "And you went on and lived. Where did you live your life, Mary?"

Eva: "We moved far away and changed our names."

Dick: "Why did you change your name?"

Eva: "People. People knew."

Dick: "People knew that the survivors of the Donner Party ate other people?"

Eva: "Yes."

Dick: "And condemned them for it."

Eva: "Yes."

Dick: "And what did you feel about that? What did you feel in being one of the survivors of that wagon train, and having eaten the people. Is this something you dealt with all your life?"

Eva: "I felt I never wanted to eat meat again, never. Then I always knew it was wrong."

Dick: "It was wrong to eat the people."

Eva: "Yeah. I shouldn't have eaten any of them."

Dick: "You were a 10-year-old child, and your momma told you it was all right. Did that not make any difference? You still felt it was really wrong?"

Eva: "My grandfather, especially. Especially him. Yeah. It was wrong."

Dick: "Did your brothers and sisters survive, Mary?"

Eva: "Yeah. But they all moved away. We never wanted to talk to each other after that."

Dick: "You never wanted to talk to each other?"

Eva: "No. We all moved different ways, and lost contact. We just didn't want anybody to know us, we didn't even want to know each other."

Dick: "Did anyone ever know again? Your husband?"

Eva: "No."

Dick: "You never told him?"

Eva: "No. I never told anybody."

Dick: "So, this is something you've repressed your entire life. Was this not a terrible burden, Mary?"

Eva: "It still is. I still feel it. I'm afraid to die."

Dick: "Why are you afraid to die?"

Eva: "I'm afraid to see my grandfather."

Dick: "Tell me about that."

Eva: "If there is a ... you know ... heaven and hell and ... he might come."

Dick: "Do you think he is going to blame a little 10-year-old girl? He might have felt good about the fact that he was able to help keep you alive. Don't you think that is possible?"

Eva: "I'm just afraid to find out. I don't know. My mother always told me that, what you say."

Dick: "She told you what?"

Eva: "That it didn't matter. That he had died anyway."

Dick: "After you were grown, did you also lose contact with your mother?"

Eva: "No. She died after that. She never got well again."

Dick: "She never got well after the winter?"

Eva: "No. She didn't. I don't think she wanted to live any more after that."

Dick: "What about your father? Was he waiting for you on the other side of the mountain or not?"

Eva: "No. I think he disowned us when he found out. I don't know."

Dick: "All right. What I want you to do now, I'm going to count from one to three, and on the count of three, you're going to be in spirit. You will have left the physical body in this incarnation, and you'll be in spirit. There will be no pain, and no emotion." (Instructions given.) "You've left the physical body. Look around, Mary. Can you see your physical body?"

Eva: "I'm floating over it."

Dick: "Yeah, okay. All right, now you are in spirit, and I want you to move forward in time a little way until you're contacted by someone else. So move forward in time, and tell me when someone else is there—if they're communicating anything to you."

Eva: "Yeah."

Dick: "Who's there?"

Eva: "My mother."

Dick: "Your mother. All right, what is she saying, or what is she impressing on your mind?"

Eva: "To come with her."

Dick: "So go with her. And I want you to continue to communicate with me. I want you to tell me what you experience."

Eva: "Well, for a while I don't want to go with her because I am afraid to see my grandfather. But she says that I can see for myself that he is there, I should, you know, it will be all right. So, after a while, I go with her. I don't know how long, and I meet my grandfather again. But he doesn't look like he did before."

Dick: "Does he look younger?"

Eva: "Yeah! And I can't believe it's my grandfather. Maybe he changed his body because we ate his."

Dick: "Okay, are you communicating with your grandfather?"

Eva: "He says that's okay, that he did die for us so we could eat."

Dick: "He died for you to keep you alive, knowing on a superconscious level exactly what he was doing."

Eva: "Right."

Dick: "Okay, does that help, Mary?"

Eva: "It helps a lot. But all the others. I don't think we always had their permission, you know? I think our mothers just decided for them."

Dick: "All right. Now listen to me carefully. I want you

105

to move forward in time to the time shortly before you were reborn as Eva. The time when you were planning this incarnation. Now, considerable time passed on the other side before you were reborn. Many years. So let's move now to the time when you were planning this life. I want to perceive the necessity of planning a life in which you needed to be always hungry, symbolically and literally." (Instructions given.)

Eva: "I was going to be stronger, and I was going to be able to control what I do and I always knew I should not have done that. It's just something that I knew, I still do know that. I should not have done that. So I needed to be hungry."

Dick: "To condemn yourself to an entire lifetime of hunger?"

Eva: "You're right ... that's stupid. Everybody's trying to tell me this, you know. Everybody's trying to tell me this."

Dick: "Everybody's trying to tell you what? Everybody on the other side is trying to tell you that this is stupid?"

Eva: "Yes."

Dick: "And you're not listening Why aren't you listening?"

Eva: "I don't know. Why do I feel guilty? Why?"

Dick: "Well, as a very young child, you were obviously impressed that it was wrong. Was your party religious? Did you have any strong religious feeling?"

Eva: "Yeah, we were very religious. But the whole world condemned us, too. Maybe I thought it was important what they thought, I don't know. We had to hide, and we had to change our names, and everybody thought we were inhuman."

Dick: "And so, even in spirit, they're telling you that it's ridiculous. You do not need to experience this."

Eva: "That's true."

Dick: "Yet you condemned yourself to that. All right. Now that's obvious, and that's what you're experiencing at this point in time. What I want you to do now, Eva, is to rise above all this." (Instructions given for Higher-Self level transfer.)

"Eva, you condemned yourself to the life that you're now living, and you have more knowledge about that now. Eva, how do you let go of this? Isn't it time that you let go? A 10-year-old child did what her mother told her to do. Even if your mother had had nothing to do with it, it would not have been wrong for you to have eaten what was served to you to survive. Now you understand this intellectually ... you don't seem able to understand it emotionally. You have no reason to feel guilt, and if you do feel the guilt, you've certainly paid the price. Look what you've put yourself through, Eva. Fifty years of starvation. Have you not paid the price? I want you to speak up now and I want you to tell me. ..."

Eva: "I have been a victim of false reality."

Dick: "Eva, you have the power and ability to let go of this self-punishment. Your subconscious mind is probably programmed to control your glands, which is a standard way of enacting karma. You can now cause this condition to return to normal so that you can eat the same diet that anyone else can eat without gaining weight. Obviously, you need to drop the weight; that's the first priority. And this will be much easier now. You can release yourself, Eva. You no longer need to punish yourself for something you had no reason to feel guilty about in the first place. In your own words, you were a victim of your own false reality. Are you fully aware of all this, Eva?"

Eva: "Yes, I am aware of this. I am free!"

Followup

Eva came to the United States in 1953 and never studied our history. She has no conscious memory of ever having heard of the Donner Party. Yet history tends to support the details of her regression:

There were a total of 87 people in the wagon train that crossed the Rockies. They crossed in three sections; the third section was the Donner Party. On the night of October 31, 1846, the first and second section arrived at a cabin on what is now known as Donner Lake. There they were trapped by early snowstorms and built two more crude cabins.

The third section, led by George Donner, wasn't as fortunate. They were caught by the storms five miles east at Alder Creek. They pitched tents, reinforcing them with ox skins. (The wagons had been previously abandoned.) The snowstorms piled 12-foot drifts on top of them, forcing the occupants to dig holes to the top, just as Eva described. They covered the tops of these holes with rags to keep out the snow and cold air.

From the three wagon train sections, 47 survived, mostly women and children. Eva was obviously among those at Alder Creek, of which eight survived, including two men.

13.

The Twenty Primary Universal Laws
By Dick Sutphen

From an article in MASTER OF LIFE magazine.

The Universe is perfectly balanced by natural and moral laws which are regulatory vibrations to maintain order. When you work within the Laws, you can be assured of an eventual positive outcome. When the Laws are transgressed, you can be assured of suffering, the only purpose of which is to teach you a better way.

1.
The Law of Harmony

This law supersedes even the fundamental Law of Karma, for Harmony is the supreme potential of balance. The purpose of karma is to attain harmony. If you throw a rock into a pond, you disturb the harmony of the pond. You are the cause and the effect is the splash and the ripples that flow out and back until the harmony is restored. Similarly, your disharmonious karmic actions flow out into the universe and back upon you, lifetime after lifetime, until eventually, your own harmony is restored. So, as you experience your life, you and the entire universe are experiencing the karmic "ripples" which will eventually result in harmony.

Once you have evolved to the position of living an entire lifetime in "harmony," you are free from the wheel of reincarnation.

2.
The Law of Reincarnation and Karma

Until you have resolved your karma and fulfilled your dharma, you will continue to reincarnate into sequential lifetimes upon the earth. Neither God nor the Lords of Karma bestow suffering upon you during these lives. You, and you alone, decide what you most need to learn in your earthly sojourns. And, for each life experience, you seek out other souls—often with shared histories, and always with karmic configurations matching your needs.

Whenever you act with intention, you create karma. (Actions are considered to be thoughts, emotions, words, and deeds, and the motive, intent, and desire behind each.) Disharmonious acts must be balanced in the future in this life, or in a future lifetime. They are rooted in fear-based emotions which must be resolved before you can release yourself from the wheel of reincarnation. You return lifetime after lifetime to test yourself, to see if you have learned your lessons. Until you can go through an entire lifetime with total involvement and no disharmonious attachment whatsoever, you will continue to reincarnate. In other words, when you can live a life of perfect "harmony," liberation will follow.

3.
The Law of Wisdom

Wisdom erases karma. If you have the wisdom to learn your lessons through love and wisdom, you can mitigate your suffering. Sadly, we seem to learn fastest through pain—through directly experiencing the consequences of our actions. As an example: You greedily take from others, and instead of learning through wisdom and love that this is wrong, you have to directly experience someone greedily taking from you, whether later in this life or in a future lifetime.

As another way to look at the Law of Wisdom, when you move toward a predestined test in your life, if you have the wisdom to proceed with harmony, you will surely mitigate the traumatic impact of the event.

Example 1: In your last life, you were married to the soul who is your mate today and whom you cruelly left for another in that previous lifetime. Before you were born into your current life, you agreed to be left by your mate under similar circumstances. This will allow you to balance your karma and directly experience the pain of abandonment. If, through the wisdom of Master of Life awareness, it is easier to consciously detach from the relationship with love, you will ease the pain of parting while also passing your own test.

Example 2: Assume that you have astrologically destined a severe relationship test for May of your 35th year. If you have learned, through past-life awareness as well as present-life learning, to be positive, non-judgmental, and without expectations in your relationship, you may only experience an argument with your mate on that fateful day in May. But if you haven't learned your past lessons and have intensified the disharmony during your relationship, you might experience a divorce in May of your 35th year.

Example 3: In several past lives, you were so proud that you were unwilling to accept any assistance from others. Pride is fear, so in this life you have astrologically predestined an event which will cause you to be institutionalized for many years. On a soul level, you decided you needed to create circumstances which would force you to subdue your pride and allow others to give to you. But through wisdom in this life, you have overridden your pride and opened your heart, gladly accepting assistance from others. Because of this, you will not have to be institutionalized to learn your lesson. Wisdom will have erased the karma.

4.
The Law of Grace

Karma can be experienced to the letter of the law or in mercy and grace. In other words, if you give love, mercy and grace to others, you will receive the same in return.

Example 1: You have destined a future event in which you will be the victim of slander and gossip which will ruin your career. But in the years preceding this event, you have become so kind and loving to other human beings, it is obvious to your Higher-Self that you have learned your needed lesson. So, the predestined event will be mitigated to the point of having little or no effect upon you.

Example 2: In a previous lifetime, you were a person of great wealth, which you used selfishly for your own and your family's indulgence. In this life, you have destined yourself to experience monetary need. But you are so giving with the little you do have, you release yourself from this self-imposed bondage and once again rise monetarily, always sharing what you have with those in need.

5.
The Law of Soul Evolution

Everyone on earth shares the goal of soul evolution, whether they realize it or not. We have reincarnated because we desire to spiritually evolve, by rising above all our fear-based emotions and learning to express unconditional love. In so doing, we raise our vibrational rate and move closer to a state of harmony.

Even when it appears that we are not evolving, we are, in reality, making progress. We learn through the pain of our disharmonious acts, which can be viewed as our mistakes or failures. But if you fell off a bicycle nine times before you learned to ride it on your tenth attempt, you needed nine failures to achieve your final success. In reality, every failure was a small success, bringing you closer to accomplishing your goal.

6.
The Law of the Bodhisattva

"Bodhisattva" is a Sanskrit term commonly accepted by most metaphysical adepts today. It means one who has transcended the need of earthly incarnations but who has chosen to return to the earth to support others in achieving enlightenment. A Bodhsattva knows he will never really be free until all souls are free. Most serious students of metaphysics have entered the "Bodhisattva Development Stage" of their evolution.

7.
The Law of Vibrational Attainment

The entire universe operates on the same principle of vibrational energy. When Einstein discovered that "matter is energy," he opened the door to merging science and metaphysics. The scientists have proven that energy cannot die, it can only transform (reincarnate). And, by its very nature, energy must move forward or backward. It cannot stand still, for to do so is stagnation, resulting in transformation.

You are energy. Your skin, which appears solid, is actually trillions of swiftly moving molecules orbiting each other at a specific vibrational rate: a physical life rate you have earned in the past as a result of how harmoniously or disharmoniously you have lived your past lives and your current life up until this moment in time. When you are harmonious for a lifetime, you will have attained the highest vibrational rate—the God level.

8.
The Law of Free Will

The Law of Free Will operates in three ways:

1. Although many of the major events in your life are astrologically predestined, you always have free will to mitigate the impact of the event, or to transcend it entirely. This will result from how you live your life up to the situation you have destined for yourself to experience. If you give grace and mercy to others, are positive, loving and compassionate, and demonstrate by your actions that you have learned past lessons, you can minimize disharmonious experiences.

2. As you obtain **Master of Life** awareness and develop conscious detachment, you will be far less affected by worldly events than in the past. A **Master of Life** enjoys all the warmth and joy that life has to offer, but detaches from the negativity by allowing it to flow through him without affecting him.

3. You always have free will in how you respond to any situation. If you respond with positive emotions, compassion and integrity, you have probably learned your karmic lessons and will not have to experience a similar situation in the future.

9.
The Law of One

Every soul, living and discarnate, is connected at the level of the collective unconscious, deep within the Higher-Self. We are all part of a great energy gestalt called God. And because we are part of God, we are God. It is the goal of the gestalt to move the energy forward, creating more energy. So, in living harmoniously, we each increase our vibrational rate and intensify the vibration of the entire gestalt. And when we are disharmonious, we decrease the vibration of the entire gestalt. Because we are one, everything you think, say and do, and the motive, intent and desire behind everything you think, say and do, affects every other soul.

10.
The Law of Manifestation

Everything manifest begins as a thought, an idea. Ideas and experiences create beliefs which, in turn, create your reality. If you are unhappy with your current reality, you must change your beliefs and your behavior.

Beliefs can be changed when you recognize those that are not working for you, and begin programming what will create success and harmony in your life. The unlimited creative power of your mind, through dedication, awareness and training, can be the wisdom to rise above your karma. Within physical and spiritual laws, you can manifest any reality you desire to experience.

In regard to changing your behavior, you must decide which disharmonious behavior you want to eliminate. Then be aware that you don't have to change how you feel about something to affect it, if you are willing to change what you are doing.

11.
The Law of Conscious Detachment

Buddha's earthly teachings are best summarized with one of his statements, "It is your resistance to **what is** that causes your suffering." And by suffering, he meant everything that doesn't work in your life: relationship problems, loss of loved ones, loneliness, sickness, accidents, guilt, monetary hardship, unfulfilled desires, and so on.

When you accept **what is,** you accept the unalterable realities in your life without resisting them. Some things are facts. They exist, and no matter how much you resist them, there is nothing you are going to be able to do about them. Change what you can change but have the wisdom to accept unalterable situations as they are without wasting mental or physical energy attempting to change what you cannot change.

Out of this acceptance comes involved detachment. The ability to enjoy all the positive aspects of life but to allow the negativity to flow through you without resistance and without affecting you.

12.
The Law of Gratitude

From the perspective of karma and the Law of One, the more you give, the more you will receive. The more you assist others, the more you assist yourself. The power of this law also works in your day-to-day life.

13.
The Law of Fellowship

When two or more people of similar vibrations are gathered for a shared purpose, their combined energy directed to the attainment of that purpose is doubled, tripled, quadrupled or more. This esoteric awareness has been used by covens, esoteric religions, healing groups, and recently, worldwide meditations for world peace.

14.
The Law of Resistance

That which you resist you draw to you, and you will perpetuate its influence upon your life. Resistance is fear, so it is something you need to karmically resolve. The Law of Resistance assures that you let go of the fear by encountering it until you are forced to deal with it by learning conscious detachment.

Example 1: You are extremely resistant toward your

116

mother-in-law, resulting in constant conflicts with her. When you attain **Master of Life** awareness and stop resisting her, by consciously detaching from the negativity, the problem will be resolved. Most disharmonious situations are solved through a change in viewpoint. By changing your perspective, you can usually eliminate the effects of a problem. And if you are no longer affected by a problem, you no longer have a problem, although nothing about the problem situation may have changed.

Another aspect of the Law of Resistance states, that which you resist, you become. If not in this lifetime, in a future incarnation.

Example 2: You have a strong resistance toward people of the Asian race. Your resistance is fear, and the quickest way to overcome fear is to directly experience that which you find so fearful. Thus you will reincarnate as an Asian in a future lifetime.

15.
The Law of Attraction

"Where your attention goes, your energy flows." You attract what you are and that which you concentrate upon. If you are negative, you draw in and experience negativity. If you are loving, you draw in and experience love. You can attract to you only those qualities you possess. So, if you want peace and harmony in your life, you must become peaceful and harmonious.

16.
The Law of Reflection

This law says that the traits you respond to in others, you recognize in yourself, both positive and negative. It has four primary manifestations: 1. That which you admire in others you recognize as existing within yourself; 2. That which you resist and react to strongly in others is sure to be found within yourself: 3. That which you resist and react to in others is something which you are afraid exists within you; and 4. That which you resist in yourself, you will dislike in others.

In other words, you have chosen to incarnate upon the manifest plane to learn to rise above the effects of fear. Those fears will always be reflected in your reactions to others, thus your goals are very obvious once you recognize how to perceive them. As you let go of the fear, you automatically open to expressing more unconditional love.

17.
The Law of Unconditional Love

The expression of unconditional love will eventually result in harmony. Unconditional love is not romantic love. It is the acceptance of others as they are without judgment or expectations. It is total acceptance of others without attempting to change them, except by our own positive example.

The Law of Unconditional Love says, "If you go out of your way to express unconditional love, you automatically rise above fear. And, as you transcend your fears, you automatically open to the expression of unconditional love."

18.
The Law of Magnetic Affinities

By astrologically choosing the time and place of your birth, you determine the nature of the effects you will experience in your life.

On the other side, before we are born, we make decisions about the lifetime we will be entering into. You chose your parents, other souls to interact with you, and the astrological configurations of your birth which determine your character, personality, abilities, restrictions, and timing for strengths and weaknesses.

If all of this seems too complicated to be real, be aware that you are only using five to ten percent of the capacity of your brain. And the brain/mind researchers say the human brain has 200,000 times the capacity of the greatest computer ever built. Such calculations as I've just described would be no problem for such a computer.

19.
The Law of Abundance

You have within yourself everything required to make your earthly incarnation a paradise if you choose to accept that which is your divine birthright. We live in a Universe of abundance, although the majority of those populating our planet appear to view it as a Universe of scarcity.

20.
The Law of Divine Order

If you seek to understand The Law of Divine Order, study the natural balance of nature, for it works very much the same way. Everything is as it should be, although mankind (our energy gestalt) is far from experiencing its potential of total harmony. There are no accidents. Your energy, translated into thoughts, words, emotions, and deeds, causes **all** your experiences. This assures that you always have the learning opportunities you require to resolve your karma. And, as with you, the collective thoughts, words, emotions, and deeds of mankind create the environment for us all.

If enough souls focus their energy upon peace, we will have peace. If the majority of souls are filled with anger, we may all have to experience war. We are all **one**, and like the many subpersonalities within you, the dominant traits of mankind (the entire gestalt) will emerge to resolve our group karma.

At this moment, a Born-Again Christian evangelist preaches fear from a pulpit in West Virginia while a yoga instructor directs a loving group meditation in Oregon. One is directing the energy of the gestalt into disharmony, the other into harmony. Hopefully, at least one can cancel out the other. If we can't attain harmony, maybe we can balance the disharmony. Certainly, as New Agers, we must not give up, individually or collectively. As always, fear is the problem and love is the answer.

*Your resistance
to what is
causes your
suffering.*

That's it.

It's very simple.

There are no exceptions.

14.
Create Your Own Reality

"Create your own reality" is the premise my work and communications have been based upon since the early '70s—so it is the ideal concept to end this introductory volume of teachings.

You have beliefs which have formed your reality. These beliefs generated the thoughts and emotions which created all your experiences. **This is why your life is exactly the way it is! You and you alone created your own reality with your beliefs.**

How does this fit in with karma? Even your present karma is the result of your past beliefs. Many of your present beliefs are based upon events from past lives. Some of these causative events are probably working for you and some may be working against you. Since karma is self-inflicted, the disharmonious effects can only be resolved by self-forgiveness. And this can only result from changing your beliefs about yourself.

If you want your current reality to be other than it is, **you must change your beliefs.** Your beliefs are not hidden deep in your subconscious mind. They are part of your conscious awareness, although they may be unexamined because you accept them as facts. Most of the things you accept as facts are actually beliefs.

It is easy to recognize your religious and political beliefs, but more difficult to pin down the core beliefs that create all aspects of your life: your weight, health, relationships, job/career, success, and creative expression.

Hypnosis, subliminals and sleep-programming self-help tapes are very popular. Why? Because the tapes assist people to reprogram their beliefs about themselves. Your disharmonious beliefs are like walls surrounding you and restricting your life. But if you desire to tear down these walls, you must first recognize their existence—and that you are not free. You can't change what you don't recognize.

In closing, I suggest that you examine your beliefs in every area of your life. Decide which are working **for** you and which are **restricting** you. If you believe people can't be trusted, your experience is they can't. If you believe you can only attain limited success, it is all you've attained. If you believe no one has an ideal relationship, you don't have an ideal relationship. If you believe sex can only be so good, that's all it is for you.

Keep in mind that you cannot become what you resent. If you believe wealthy people are snobs, you will never allow yourself to have money. You always live up to your self-image, but it can work against you. If rich people are snobs, how could you allow yourself to become a snob? Replace your negative thoughts with a positive statement, such as, "I think wealthy people are in a wonderful position to do good with their money."

Are you overweight and resentful of those with an ideal body? Do you wish you had a fulfilling relationship and resent those who do? Do you dream of success while resenting those who have made it? **It is time to change your beliefs by recognizing disharmonious thoughts and replacing them with a harmonious thought in support of your desires. You can create your own reality!**

122

Write for a free copy of *Master of Life* magazine. It contains news and articles on the subjects of reincarnation, psychic exploration and self-help, in addition to complete information on all Sutphen Seminars and over 300 self-help and self-exploration tapes from Valley of the Sun Publishing: hypnosis, meditation, sleep programming, subliminal programming, and New Age music.

Valley of the Sun Publishing
Box 38
Malibu, California 90265
818/889-1575

Valley of the Sun New Age Tapes

Dick Sutphen's books and tapes are available in most metaphysical/New Age stores, or you may obtain them directly from Valley of the Sun Publishing, Box 38, Malibu, CA 90265. Add $1.50 per order for shipping and handling. The following is a partial list of our line of over 300 titles which includes Hypnosis, Meditation, Sleep Programming, Subliminal Programming, Symbol Therapy, Children's Programming, and New Age Music. For additional information, you may call 818/889-1575.

How To Be A Better Receiver In Hypnosis
Side A: Workshop/Lecture
Side B: Hypnosis Sessions

Two intense hours of lectures, exercises and special sessions designed to maximize your hypnosis receptivity. Anyone can learn to receive hypnotic impressions well, once they understand the various methods and do the exercises on this tape. Increases effectiveness of past-life regressions, higher-self explorations or other hypnosis work.

Single tape audio cassette. . HP042—$12.50

Breaking The Chains of Illusion
A Condensed Book On Two Tapes
By Dick Sutphen

Enlightenment is freedom. Enlightenment is realization of your true nature. And for those who follow a Master of Life path, there is a vast region to be found within oneself where there is no recrimination ... where you can attain freedom from self and an awareness that you are truly a part of God. Two tapes in a vinyl album with a beautiful color cover.

.... N104—$14.95

Know Thy Higher Self
By Dick Sutphen

An intensive seminar on reincarnation and karma, this four-tape album is an explanation of metaphysics from a Reincarnationists' viewpoint. Covers the Supreme Universal Law; What Is, Is; The 7 Karmic Paths, 7 Dharmic Directions & 7 Soul Goals; Vibrational Rates & Astral Levels; Reincarnation, the Way It Really Is; 15 Tenets to End Suffering & Evolve Spiritually; Meditations; much, much more. If you sincerely want to end suffering, evolve spiritually and rise above your karma, the wisdom on these tapes can completely change your life. Instruction manual included. ....RA201—$45.00

Your Only Help Is Self-Help
A Condensed Book on Two Tapes
By Dick Sutphen

You can be your own best therapist. This condensed book on tape gives you the information you need to create a brand-new reality—fast! These tapes are for anyone whose life isn't working. You don't have to change how you feel about something or someone to affect it if you are willing to change what you are doing. This two-hour self-exploration is the equivalent of a full one-day seminar. Two tapes in a vinyl album. .... N101—$14.95

Viewing Past Lives
The Ascension Technique
By Dick Sutphen

A unique meditation technique of past-life regression that always works! This album uses a gentle meditative body relaxation, followed by the "Ascension Technique" instructions. You don't regress—you go directly back to the past life. It is powerful and it works! You'll experience your past lives before your inner eyes. The sessions in this album offer a wide new range of explorations: pre-birth decisions about your life, past-life patterns, karmic traits and soul goals. Use alone or in a group. 4 tapes in a vinyl album with instruction manual. ....C833—$39.95

Psychic Powers Programming
By Dick Sutphen

This fantastic album includes a great "how-to" book by W. E. Butler explaining step-by-step exactly what you need to know to use these awareness-expanding techniques. On the cassette tapes, Dick uses his most effective techniques to program you to open and develop in each of the four areas. Each tape can be used as hypnosis or as sleep programming. The four areas covered are Aura Reading; Psychometry; Telepathic Ability; and Clairvoyance. 4 tapes, instruction manual & book. .... C832—$32.95

Past-Life Therapy
By Dick Sutphen

All your feelings, anxieties, hang-ups, fears, and phobias come from some event or series of events in your past. Our research shows this includes prior incarnations. Dick Sutphen has trained mental health professionals to use these awareness-expanding techniques with their patients to eliminate problems by getting to the cause, either from this life or a past life. Thousands of people have used these hypnosis regression techniques to experience their past lives. Two-tape album includes instruction manual. .... AX901—$29.95

Your Inner Temple
By Dick Sutphen

This spiritual album has been created in response to hundreds of requests from seminar participants who have loved sessions like these. Each tape in this 2-tape album uses Dick's "Chakra Balancing Meditation Induction," which takes you deeper than any induction he has ever used. Even more important, you are awakened experiencing an incredible balance and harmony. Ancient methodologies combined with contemporary awareness in directed meditations to grow and evolve spiritually. Includes instruction manual. .... C843—$24.95

Circle of Light
By Dick Sutphen

Directed meditations to open to more intense spiritual awareness, integrating the power of ancient ritual into your life. If you are ready to open to more intense spiritual awareness and integrate the power of ancient ritual into your life, this album will take you on your next step to becoming a Master. This two-tape album uses Dick's "Chakra Balancing Meditation Induction," and comes with an instruction manual. .... **C842—$24.95**

Soulmates
By Dick Sutphen

Would you like to meet your twin soul—your perfect partner? You and your twin soul usually share a lifelong relationship which allows you both to more easily fulfill your life goals. This 2-tape album uses the most powerful techniques to assist you in finding this person. It contains meditations to direct your Higher Self to meet your soulmate and to check out an individual you feel might be a soulmate. One tape contains subliminal messages hidden behind music to assist your subconscious mind to find your twin soul. Album comes with 100-page instruction manual. .... **C835—$29.95**

Sedona: Psychic Energy Vortexes
Book By Dick Sutphen

A 180-page trade-sized paperback book on Sedona, Arizona—location of a vortex energy center that enhances all psychic abilities. Thousands of people have had incredible metaphysical experiences here, ranging from direct contact with spirits, visions, weight loss, and healings to strange manifestations and effects. A fascinating exploration of psychic abilities and the unlimited power of the mind. .... **B922—$7.95**

127

Master of Life Manual
By Dick Sutphen

Past lives to human-potential principles—a complete manual of the basic communications to begin to create your own reality NOW. Newly revised and updated for 1987, the material makes the book much more powerful than before. It includes a major section on how the mind works and the basics of the Master of Life philosophy. A classic! Quality paperback. .... **B963—$3.95**

Enlightenment Transcripts
By Dick Sutphen

This book takes up where **Master of Life Manual** leaves off. Thirty-six fast-reading dialogues simplify complicated concepts so they become more easily understood, providing eye-opening, human-potential awareness while weaving the reader through powerful examples of karma and past-life therapy. Quality paperback. .... **B923—$3.95**

Past-Life Therapy In Action
By Dick Sutphen & Lauren Leigh Taylor

A life-changing book that explores many exciting case histories right out of the Sutphen Seminar's training room or from Dick's research-gathering one-to-one hypnotic regression sessions. The authors carefully show the **cause**, the **effect** and the **karmic lesson**, plus they provide human-potential awareness of how to rise above the undesirable effects. Newly revised, 1987 edition. Large trade-sized paperback. **B915—$7.95**